OLD
RARE
NEW

THE INDEPENDENT
RECORD SHOP

black dog
publishing

london uk

For Kevin

TABLE OF CONTENTS

FOREWORD

Barry Seven

Buying second hand records started, for me, at aged 12, in Soho, London, at Cheapo Cheapo Cheapo, a record shop that's still there and so is it's owner. Everytime I see him I see how I've aged along side him. Record store owners are all the same, that madness that oozes out of their skin and perfumes their shops. The weight of vinyl on their shoulders and the overbearing fear that the record in your hand is the future, and they missed it—but only price-wise. Cheapo's was like a Venus Flytrap, in keeping with all the clip joints and girly shows that made that area of London famous. The owner would write the price on the cover in ballpoint pen, on a sticker covering the same amount—a crime to the collector, but I've never been a collector, so who cares. It's the music contained therein that matters. His act of defacing each record secretly showed his contempt for, in his mind, the rubbish he sold the gullible punter. This con and counter-con has always fascinated me. Do record shop owners hate what they sell? Or is it that they like us? We all have piles upon piles of our glorious mistakes tucked away in dark corners, which far outweigh our victories. In those days, I'd buy anything that looked interesting. It's hard to say what defines interesting—just the fact that it's alone, lost in the back, covered in dust. A gem in the dirt, its cover as mysterious as its contents, hopefully! My first records were John Barry soundtracks and Stateside r & b compilations. Forever instrumental music, and rock 'n' roll are my basic musical DNA. Cheapo's owner would often shout at you if you transgressed a pile... for his eyes only! I now prefer a grumbling owner to one that wants to fit you up like a high-class tailor or tries to show you his recent acquisitions, which sadly are going home with him.

I guess the best time I had record hunting was, strangely, Jarvis Cockers stag-do. We were all record hunters, all friends for years and possibly all responsible for fostering our dodgy finds on YOU. We swooped down on Portsmouth for the day like the Magnificent Seven, but probably looked more like the Dirty Dozen, and held sway in the numerous record shops in that god-forsaken town. Needless to say, it was a very gentlemanly affair, like an old ladies cookery class with loads of hints and tips and admiring displays of knowledge and musical generosity. Looking back we found records that shaped our individual futures. The very act of shopping is DOING and that's why I can't bear the Internet, as it's the act of looking. Why do men love lists so much? The record shop in all its battered piles and categories is, for me at least, a social act. A parlay with the past and what mates you have left behind.

Touring with Add N to (X) in America was a feverish exercise—PD's spent recklessly in pre-Internet heaven. Stocks so vast you broke out in a sweat, especially in San Francisco or Acadamy in New York. In those pre-Internet, non-monetised days you knew that the staff in those places hadn't censored what you saw because of the 'pile it high and flog it cheap' ethic. To my shame, I was given thousands of records by a mom and pop store outside Detroit. Lots of shit I promise. I waited until I got to the Texas desert to dispatch them one by one with a shotgun. The Allman Brothers have never sounded so good exploding with buckshot in those vast and lonely skies. And I have never been so shocked as I was at my natural ability with a gun.

So finally, spare a thought for the store-owners themselves. A sobering story recounted to me from one such store-working perennial optimist, found him buying stock for his shop from two extremely obese men whose miniscule apartment was wall to wall records. So many records in fact that the piles had formed themselves around their owners gelatinous bodies. The smell was rank and my friend excused himself and went to their toilet, which stank and was crammed to the ceiling with records—whereupon he noticed a large broom. Curious, he inquired to the two housebound, obese gentlemen, why they had a broom in their toilet? The reply—"to wipe our arses, idiot!". He left in disgust. And the moral of the tale is that the shop owner has to go to greater depths than us, casual bargain hunters, for stock, which accounts for their Jesus-like tolerance of our myopic lust, or thier pure hatred. We will never know the depths they had to plumb.

Barry Seven is one of the original members of pioneering British electronics-and-synths outfit Add N to (X). He now runs Horseglue Records, an imprint of Mute Records.

Signage from Gramaphone, Chicago, Illinois

KEEP YOUR FINGERS OFF THE GROOVES AND PUT THE RECORDS BACK IN THEIR PAPER SLEEVES

SIMON SINGLETON

For a small shop, we've crammed a hell of a lot of people inside at times! And I think that's what people will remember most fondly about the current incarnation of Pure Groove—our new, larger, premises will open in June 2008. Yup, there was the day when a hundred people (and a gorilla—don't ask) squeezed inside to watch Supergrass (while many, many more peered through the glass) and the chilly wintery night when Mystery Jets played two gigs because so many people turned up. Sometimes an absolute nightmare to organise, in-stores are rarely anything but a treat to host.

Brief history I guess. Well, we opened in 1989, importing the kind of early dance records that were gold dust to the burgeoning dance music community. Next, we set up some labels, including Locked On (which signed The Streets) won Record Shop of the Year twice, and started opening the store to an ever-wider spectrum of music. That's nearly 20 years of music in two sentences! You don't want to read a press release after all.

What tunes do we hold dearest? Well, naturally too many to mention—"Has it Come to This" by The Streets will always be special, the first record by Bromheads Jacket which sold out in a day and now sells on eBay for hundreds, and Sebastian Tellier's otherworldly *La Ritournelle*, which brings a collective tear to our eye, continues to sell to this day and even sound-tracked one Pure Groover's wedding walk.

We're moving to Farringdon in Central London to spread our wings into a more diverse selection of music-related goodies—we'll miss our North London abode greatly, but we know that the best times are ahead.

Simon Singleton runs celebrated dance music record store, Pure Groove, based in Archway, North London. Pure Groove is also a record label and publishing company.

Etherea Records, Manhattan, New York

TO HAVE AND TO HOLD:
AN INCOMPLETE GUIDE
TO INDEPENDENT RECORD
SHOPS IN AMERICA

Emma Pettit

Once the fancy, faddish accessory of only the most pretentious and flash amongst us, it is less than ten years later that I can now count (one one hand) the number of people I know that don't own a mobile phone. Often, one that also doubles as a radio, MP3 player, Internet browser, camera, video player and football score transmitter. Even the most anti-commodity amongst us breaks out in a sweat at the realisation that their pocket life-organiser, complete with digitised back catalogue of The Cure, is still sitting on the toilet cistern back at home, and that they won't be able to rearrange the time and location of that night's social encounters five times over before a final arrangement is decided upon.

Consider the complete transformation of life as we know it through the development of the Internet, and my student experiences of being baffled at the possibilities of using an MS Dos intranet system to communicate with my tutors seem an impossibly long way in the past. Now, we don't even blink at the ability to shop online for groceries, book a long haul flight, donate to charity, pay household bills, research an essay, buy seven songs off an 11-track album and watch Saddam Hussein's execution, all from the comfort of the sofa. For those of us of a certain age, our everyday lives have altered beyond recognition in the last ten years, and for the most part, without much notice, as technology quietly facilitates every small aspect of our daily activity. Music, with the arrival of MySpace, iTunes, and overwhelming digital music

ownership via downloads, free online album releases, MP3s, podcasts and streaming, is perhaps one of the most significant areas of culture affected by technological developments. So much so that what was once a social, object-oriented pastime, is now very much at the mercy of wav files and tinny sonic recordings, with its associated visual identity shrinking with every new nano-sized gadget introduced on the market.

With this in mind, plus the opportunity to spend three months working on a film project, my partner Kevin and I had already agreed that independent music would be our subject, and the changing face of musical production and consumption seemed an interesting and timely bet. With its wealth of vinyl, and vast musical heritage, we thought America would give us ample opportunity to source a rich array of material. Concluding that the realm of the independent record shop was pertinent, wide-reaching, and offered a specifically human insight into the spaces of independent music, we agreed that this should be the focal subject for our film, and eventually, this book.

More than a particular band, musical genre, or local 'scene', record stores offer the potential for personal stories, explorations of communities, insights into cities and regions and the way they experience and share music. This is as much about the owner of a small, independent business as it is about delving into musical consumption as seen through the

racks of records and vinyl that still pervade every small town and big city in America, in some shape or form. Record stores are central to the flow of the musical food chain—it's where the music is put into the hands of Joe Public, the grass roots level where moments of musical discovery begin.

As we embarked on committing the vinyl store to film, record shops had been the subject of British newspaper column inches for several years: news reels claimed vinyl sales were massively on the up (over a million 7" singles were sold in Britain in 2006—whereas back in 2003, the figure sat at less than 170,000) with a renewed fashion for 'vintage' fuelling the retro and analogue fire. Yet the Internet and downloading seemed to have had a simultaneously detrimental effect on the life span of small independent shops—not to mention the music industry at large. In London alone, Stone Fish records, two branches of Reckless and several more long-standing vinyl haunts besides, had all disappeared in less than a year.

Stateside, things seemed to be following a similarly bleak pattern. Between 2003 and 2006, the official figure of small indie record stores closing during that period sat staggeringly at over 900, which is approximately 25 per cent of stores across America. At the end of 2006, Tower Records had gone bankrupt for a second and final time, and yet vinyl was also seeing some sort of a revival. In a strong moment of visual symbolism, Manhattan's independent Mecca, Other Music, stood with its doors defiantly open and the store interior bustling, as the East Fourth Street branch of Tower right opposite, got rid of the final dregs in its bargain bins and permanently closed its doors.

In addition to the feeling that the record shop world was contracting, if not disappearing entirely, we were also aware of the gradual loss of physical spaces and objects—record shops and albums with artwork in our case—that we wanted to explore. What does it mean to own less things, for them all to virtually centre around one digital object, to lose the visual identity around music and musicians, and the physical ritual of putting on a record.

It was these questions and contradictions, which we hoped to explore in our film, alongside a more general celebration of the communities and musical experiences that these stores offer up. Several months, rolls of film and wonderfully eclectic stories later—featuring a series of pit-stops in New York, Boston, Detroit, Ann Arbor, San Francisco, Los Angeles and Chicago— our vinyl round-trip has also been committed to this book.

Researching the wealth of small independent record stores in Manhattan—our starting point for the trip—included some invaluable assistance in the form of Tim Broun, a friend of a friend and human encyclopaedia when it comes to the last 20 years of New York's alternative music scene. His local knowledge, contacts and general enthusiasm for our project were incredible, he hooked us up with a host of stores, venues, DJs and New York's resident music enthusiasts, each of whom seemed to want to be involved in our project and each of whom possessing another set of ideas for people we should talk to and places we should explore.

Tim initially took us on a walking tour of downtown Manhattan—we spent several hours strolling from Greenwich Village on the west side, over to the East Village, taking in over a dozen stores along the way, including Subterranean Records on Cornelia Street, where Patti Smith has spent downtime. The owner was described, on one vinyl junkie blog, as the "chain-smoking unholy spawn of Lou Reed and Bob Dylan". Owner Michael is a much sweeter character than this suggests, and Subterranean is a shrine to all things post-punk and rock, the bins filled with multiple copies of LPs by Television, Talking Heads, Neil Young, Bowie and the Stones. We also discovered Gimme Gimme Records, on East Fifth Street, a second hand vinyl store from Thursday to Sunday (also stocking a great range of analogue music machines) with the same space used for teaching piano lessons during the rest of the week. The pristine Sound Library on Orchard Street, an a-typical clean and bright crate-diggers delight, hosts a wealth of rare groove, library recordings and a stash of hip hop, jazz, reggae and soul. We found up-to-the minute new releases store Etherea, run by Richard Lee, whose large 'Old Rare New' sign hung on the back wall of the store was the inspiration for the name of this book and our film. And then the double joy of Jammyland, one of Alphabet City's longest standing reggae stores (Deadly Dragon Sound being the other favoured reggae emporium on Forsyth Street), which also houses Dominic Fernow's Hospital Productions. Complete with a trap door and step ladder to gain entry, this is a tiny, meticulous red and black shrine to all things noise and black metal, with an intricate range of hand-printed EPs, DIY cassette tapes and CD-Rs, decorated with destroyed microphones and a guitar hammered to the wall with long rusty nails.

Tim's vinyl itinerary was also accompanied by an alternative sight-seeing tour of iconic musical spots—from the Gem Spa news stand, where the New York Dolls shot the back cover for their first album, to the fire escape-adorned brownstones

Top Left: The former location of CBGB, Manhattan, New York
Bottom Left: Archive of Contemporary Music, Manhattan, New York

Top Right: Old Rare New sign, Etherea Records, Manhattan, New York
Bottom Right: Etherea Records, Manhattan, New York

on Saint Marks' Place that were used on the cover of Led Zeppelin's *Physical Graffiti* LP, to a basement room where No Wave label 99 Records had their offices, to the recent grave of CBGB's, which had been sent to a better place only a few months previously. All that was left at that time was the metal skeleton of its infamous sign, and a few black and white stickers, a small memorial for a place of such creative significance for New York's music and art scenes.

We also spent a lot of time in scene-y Williamsburg, Brooklyn, across the river from Manhattan, an area which is most easily described as New York's version of the east end of London, having experienced much of the same creative influx and subsequent regeneration. Williamsburg is said to be home to the biggest artistic community in America, housing artists, musicians, and other creatives who have moved out of Manhattan due to extortionate housing prices, and now nurture a satellite community of galleries, cafes, bars, small independent shops and studios. Even now, Williamsburg is getting pricey though, and people continue to move out to areas such as Green Point, parts of Queens, and Flatbush.

Williamsburg was also home to our first record store visit proper—Marquise Dance Hall, a small store selling second hand records and books, also housing a little gallery out the back and a garden where they screen 16 mm films in the summer. Just off the main drag (Bedford Avenue) on Grand and Roebling, and run by an artist and filmmaker couple called Mark and Ayca, it had been open about a year. We interviewed Mark about the set up, the local community, and how he sourced all of the records. They specialised in a lot of folk, ethnic, free jazz, avant garde and punk, all laid out beautifully in old wooden crates and tea chests. Given the store has since closed, it also turned out to be illustrative of just how tough the independent record store business was getting, and that our trip was in some sense a rather timely recording and committing to history of some of these inspiring and unique spaces.

As we began to tour New York's record stores in earnest, it started to highlight how, when you are working on a project, everything in and around that work, and everything else besides, seems to be informed by the subject matter. We were making a film about independent record stores in America, and now everything I looked at in the street, read in the press, noted as I walked into a shop, or observed about the local neighbourhood, seemed to be viewed through the eyes of the

film. Would this corner on of the Lower East Side, make a nice flash of contextual footage to reflect the colourful, grimy-but-fashionable part of Manhattan that is home to a number of the record stores we are speaking with? How did an article I was reading in the New York press about the commercial take over of MySpace feed into the argument we were forming about the shifting terrain of the exchange of music? Should I have been photographing every small independent gig venue, musically-themed mural, or collection of stickers promoting underground music, in order to build up a wider visual landscape? Should I have been discussing the project with every single person I met, just in case they suggested a store we didn't know about, someone who'd make a great interview, or give a new angle on the subject that could really inform the narrative?

It was quite hard to switch off, and even when we weren't filming or scheduling, or reflecting on where we were with what footage, we were exchanging ideas, or, in a less overt way, thinking and considering the film. Whenever something appeared in front of us that has some connection to record stores, vinyl or independent music, it immediately resonated with the context of the film. And as well as feeding the project, these constant observations also made for a really detailed exploration of a place, and offered a compelling, alternative way to see a country. The pursuit of records, record shops, record shop owners and their customers offered up new perspectives on geography, local communities, architecture, culture, politics and people. As well as seeing things from a very specifically-channelled perspective, we were also seeing things that we might not have noticed at all, was it not for such focus.

The more people we met, the more we began to see themes starting to recur, and groups of stores and people forming. It seemed that there were three main types of record stores that we were dealing with. The first was the 'old school' original store, around for years and perhaps the most typically imagined record shop. Alongside these, the specialist stores, offering up rare groove, 78s, 7" singles, library music, supplying to narrow and niche underground music markets and servicing die-hard collectors. Finally, the new breed of record store—of which Other Music, Sound Fix, Cake Shop and Eat Records are all examples. Offering a more complex notion of musical experience, these spaces play on the traditional notion of the record store as social space, tying in live shows, ticket booking, a cafe, a bar, preview listening parties and various other ways of enticing customers into the store and its wider creative community.

Other Music is now one of the most well-known and successful independent music stores in America. On a par with London's Rough Trade shops, it does well in online business and international trade, as well as having an exceptionally good quality range of CDs and vinyl in store. With regular in-store performances, ticket purchasing options for gigs, a big notice board and a stash of the best free music and culture rags in town, it has made itself an indispensable space for independent music fans, across a host of genres.

Down the road in Soho, Cake Shop offers a select range of vinyl, CDs and a pile of DIY releases, and also has a live gig venue with a two am license in the basement, where it hosts underage clubs on Saturday afternoons—and yes, a nice line in homemade cakes and coffees out front. Sound Fix, across the water in Williamsburg, is fronted by a spacious record store, with a large cafe, bar and live space of faded grandeur out the back.

Eat Records, up a side street (Meserole Avenue) as Williamsburg meets Green Point, is another small but perfectly formed little record store cum friendly hang out. Run by Casey and Jeff, who also host a regular radio slot on East Village Radio, their skinny store serves up a range of quality vinyl, alongside homemade sandwiches, cakes and cups of tea, and has also unwittingly become home to some of Brooklyn's chess enthusiasts, another breed of obsessive convening in this musically-themed front room.

In contrast to this new breed, some of the most long-standing record stores in New York are those which have been around since the 1960s—mostly based in Greenwich Village on the lower west side of Manhattan, home to the first New York record store 'scene'. Bleecker Bob's on West Third Street has been in business since the early 1960s, and was first set up to feed Bob's own penchant for doo wop records, gradually transforming into a business, now historic for record collectors, and an example of the most stereotypical type of store you might imagine. A cluttered, jam-packed and not wholly clean space, stuffed full with crates of vinyl, all slightly dusty and musty, pasted floor to ceiling with old rock and punk posters. Records are split into sub-sections with hand-written dividers (rock, psychedelia, jazz, folk, blues, country, avant garde, punk, new wave, no wave, experimental, etc), two dollars bargain bins are scattered across the floor, rock stickers cover the cash till and counter, and a handful of scowling middle aged men, pepper the dark corners of

the store—staff and customers both. Something of a time-warp, you can't imagine this place or its management has changed much in the last few decades. The store is both a grimy treasure trove of historic treasures and new pleasures waiting to be discovered, and also slightly tired, as though it's somehow past its prime. Early excitement and proudly superior, but knowledgeable, staff assistance has given way to a feeling that everything's just a bit of an effort, that friendly customers are just trying too hard, and things, well, they just aren't like they were 'in the old days'.

Apart from Bob's, Greenwich Village probably houses a further dozen or so other stores that have been there for ages; Rebel Rebel, which has been serving up British imports and copies of the *NME* for the last 20 years or so. Vinyl Mania, dance music specialists for 28 years, were the original purveyors of Italo-disco in America, and one of the first stores to specialise in records for DJs, supplying pioneering dance music club the Paradise Garage and its resident DJ Larry Levan their wares during the late 1970s and early 80s. Vinyl Mania, run by Italian American 12" expert Charlie, also has a vinyl warehouse of mythical proportions stored out in Coney Island, which we were privileged enough to visit, and which suggested the record collecting 'sickness', as a bemused Charlie described it, can sometimes get slightly out of hand.

The fantastic House of Oldies, is run by the wonderfully film-star-esque Bob Abrahams, who has been in charge of the store for nearly 40 years, and serves up 'oldies'—mainly 45s from the 1940s, 50s, 60s and 70s, as well as a variety of other formats. He thinks there are around 700,000 pieces of vinyl inside the store itself, which is like a shoe box, and stacked floor to ceiling with an alphabetical catalogue of high quality and rare vinyl, ranging in value from $10 to $1,000. He also has a huge store room out back, and another storage space out of the city, which makes you wonder whether all of it could possibly be seen, let alone sold.

Speaking to Abrahams, who was pretty much an international celebrity of the vinyl realm—serving up music to David Bowie, John Lennon and Robert Plant over the years—it begins to illustrate what a hugely significant and comprehensive historical archive and record of contemporary music that record stores like House of Oldies offer. Not only does it satisfy and service the collections and listening pleasures of thousands of individuals, but it also celebrates and commemorates an incredible music history, format and obsession, and the

layers of popular culture, politics, fashion, technological development and social history that the mere production of a piece of vinyl can represent and chart.

As much as there are new stores and old, the record store is also symptomatic of the types of collector and record buyer that inhabit them. There is a clear distinction between those who love music, and those who love collecting. There are those who will head for the store on new releases day, attend listening preview parties and play their new record a hundred times over in order to soak up layer upon layer of new sounds, subtleties of production, and change in musical direction from their favourite recording artist. Then, there are those who will sit at their computer through the night, upping their eBay bid systematically, in order to be the owner of the hardest-to-find, pre-stereo, analogue-recorded rare groove, with the gate-fold sleeve still in pristine condition, and a slight colour defect on the label, which means that only three of this precise format exist, and it might be a bit risky to actually play it. These two breeds are pretty different species, but each is fired up by the prospect of picking up something unusual and inspiring, whether it is the emotional thrill from the opening bars of a new track, or the realisation that the limited edition, first pressing 45 you're holding actually matches the criteria outlined in your record collector manual.

Take the recent hysteria that erupted around the emergence of the mysterious Velvet Underground acetate—symbolising every crate digger and collector's idea of a holy grail. As the story goes, a record collector called Warren Hill was going through a box of records in Chelsea, New York, that someone was flogging on the sidewalk He'd picked out a couple of good bargains, when he came across another disc, looking pretty ragged, with a yellowed label reading "Velvet Underground" and the words "Attn N Dolph" on it, dated 1966. It cost him ¢75. Several phone conversations to fellow-collector friends and some more serious research time later, he discovered he had actually come across the first 'finished' version—and only surviving copy—of the LP that Andy Warhol had touted to Columbia Records, N Dolph being the record executive he had approached with the demo. Not only that, but it was the original acetate, the template used at the vinyl press as the album went into production. Much hype and media hysteria later, it just sold on eBay for over $25,000. Despite afterwards being revealed as a hoax, it clearly represents the hunger and desire in owning such a unique and unexpected object, infused with the romance and rich storytelling of musical history, and the lengths of obsession and desire for ownership.

Whether you're in it for the money, the pride, or the sonic pleasure, the collector or music-lover's habit also translates into a wealth of personal collections—walls of vinyl delight, full of prized joys, rarities, first-ever purchases, and a glorious array of colourful designs.

The music itself might be the first and last *raison d'etre* for these striking 12" squares, but there's a whole lot that sits in between. The cover art is a major part of the appeal and seduction, housing those shiny black grooves in jackets of myth, fantasy, energy and exhilaration and making them the objects of desire that infuse additional value, history and memory into the music. Not only do you get 50 minutes of sonic bliss for your fistful of dollars, but the album cover, lyrics and liner notes bring to life much more than this—from the photography, the fashion, the graphic design style to the political statement, each contribute to a sense of history and identity, a space for socially conscious humour, creative flair, protest and satire.

Amongst the personal treasure troves we infiltrated on our travels—from Bronx DJ Bazooka Joe's old school hip hop joints; Guardian journalist and San Francisco resident Sylvie Simmons' latest penchant for Elvis records, which complemented her ukulele lessons; to shelves of American hardcore belonging to writer and filmmaker Steven Blush, who also had every Black Sabbath record signed by the band members. Even Bob George's public service initiative, the Archive of Popular Music (where he is attempting to preserve two copies of every piece of popular music recorded)—finally, it was the collection of Yale Evelev that was one of the most exciting. Yale, who runs the record label Luaka Bop, owned by David Byrne (Talking Heads), houses his impressive collection of vinyl in his apartment in Soho, New York, where he has lived for 30 years. Luaka Bop celebrates music from all over the world, with Yale's theory that "anywhere I could find at least one record on vinyl that excited me, that's where I was happy to release music from"—and that has taken him across the continents, from North Africa to China, Scotland to Brazil.

His collection is therefore somewhat diverse, but his energy about his records lies in the cover designs, unusual formats and hand-made covers, as much as the music itself—though this is definitely not relegated below aesthetics, the two rather informing each other. Paper-cut, early, handmade Negativland covers sit alongside day-glo transparent Talking Heads picture discs, Chinese folks songs and a novelty miniature vinyl box-

Vinyl racks, Val's Halla, Oak Park, Chicago

set. But the moment my jaw dropped to the floor was when he explained that he'd grown up in Philadelphia, in the same town that Sun Ra had lived before moving to Chicago, and promptly revealed a pile of psychedelic hand-made covers, complete with bits of shower curtain glued to the front, that he'd picked up locally—all pre-Chicago (when the covers started to be printed by machine), one of a kind, and little pieces of history by the man from Saturn.

On leaving New York, we took an overnight train to Detroit, taking in the miles of industrial wasteland that littered its suburbs, its hundreds of abandoned 1930s car factories glistening in the soft dawn light as we drew into the eerily empty city. We were met at the train station by Cornelius Harris, one of the owners of Somewhere in Detroit, home to the Underground Resistance label, and centre of the iconic Detroit techno scene, comprising Juan Atkins, Carl Craig, Mad Mike Barnes and the rest. Somewhere in Detroit, can be found, well, somewhere in Detroit—on a non-descript downtown street, in the basement of a non-descript building that formerly housed the offices of a laundry business, but which now conceals Underground Resistance's graffiti-tagged, appointment-only boutique, the walls adorned with comments of respect and love from an array of the world's most celebrated dance music DJs and their extended family.

From downtown, Cornelius drove us to one of Detroit's original Ford factory suburbs, Dearborn, which is also where recording artist couple Windy and Carl run their beloved Stormy Records from. Their plant-filled, front room-style store sat above Green Brain Comics, together forming a little oasis of alternative and odd ball culture amongst the personality-free shopping malls and parking lots around them. Offering a wide range of the weird, the niche, the alternative and the independent, Stormy Records exudes a gentle, personal and genuine vibe, based solely on their own enthusiasm and passion for music.

After a quick, cold, stop off in Ann Arbor, Michigan, including visits to the Schoolkids in Exile record store and Matthew Dear's Ghostly Recordings label, our next extended port of call was California, arriving in San Francisco in time for a Christmas break and stay with friends. A few days into the new year, we hired a car and took a drive along the astonishing coastal panoramas of Route One down to Los Angeles, passing through the staggering natural beauty of Big Sur, national parks full of red woods, sea lion-lined beaches and the dramatic and cinematic Hearst Castle,

the momentous location for Orson Welles' 'xanadu' in Citizen Kane.

While in Los Angeles, we filmed seven interviews in two days. The excellent independent Plug Research, and one of their signings, Daedelus; Peanut Butter Wolf's indie hip hop label Stone's Throw and musical collective, production house, radio outfit and label, Dub Lab. We then interviewed four different record stores: Sea Level (a new-ish leftfield indie rock store in Silverlake), Rockaway, which has been going for nearly 30 years and specialises in collectibles and memorabilia, particularly from The Beatles and Beach Boys, and featuring everything from limited edition John and Ringo lunch boxes and promotional *Good Vibrations* skateboards, to blow up guitars and original 1960s fanzines. Atomic offers a host of vinyl, especially jazz, and Freak Beat which sells new and used CDs and vinyl, and is run by two characters called Bob and Tom.

It was at about this point that I started to notice—or rather vocalise my observations—that the music industry at large, including the record store domain, is still a very male territory. More specifically, male, middle-aged and white. Women are few and far between in this arena and the majority of people we had come across, from the store owners and their staff, to DJs, musicians, and the labels and distribution networks that sit around them, were of the male variety. No great surprise there I guess, as it's no secret that the music business has always been, and continues to be, dominated by men, but it really reinforced the fact for me in exploring the terrain. It was not that we didn't meet any female vinyl fans—we hooked up with a good few female music professionals on our travels, and it's certainly not that women aren't interested in music or vinyl, but I couldn't get past the fact that the boys out number the girls. "It's not a place to pick up women!" said co-owner Rick, at Atomic Records in Los Angeles.

Of the few women we did talk to, we were met with a host of equally obsessive and knowledgeable music aficionados, from store-owners and workers, to a label owner and producer, and another who works on re-issues for music publisher Abkco. But, they were definitely thin on the ground, and still seem to have to fight that little bit harder to claim their space in the musical realm. At Good Records in Manhattan, home to a great range of rare groove with original artwork to buy off the walls, there is even a "ladies' bench", complete with coffee table books for the vinyl widows to peruse, while their

2 INCH

male counterparts dig the crates. Thoughtful on the one hand, it does also presuppose that women couldn't possibly be interested in shopping for records themselves, and would rather flick through magazines in search of the latest lipstick shade, than scour the bins for a sound library oddity or screen-printed limited edition EP.

Dance music specialists Halcyon Records in DUMBO, Brooklyn, have acknowledged this somewhat, and host a monthly in-store event aimed at encouraging and promoting women DJs. One of their female staff, Connie, who also DJs in and around New York, brings down an array of girl DJs to the store and they hit the decks, with all women who shop in the store receiving a ten per cent discount on vinyl purchases. However, it seemed unfortunate that this even has to be the case—that women are seen somehow as a bit of a novelty on the scene. Although Halycon's strategy is an important one, and should not be discouraged, it also highlights that fact that the business of music, including record stores, is not necessarily an even playing field, and women who DJ, or collect vinyl, are viewed as the exception, rather than the norm.

Gender aside, the local independent music-store owner does a lot more than re-fill the bins and exchange cash for vinyl. Purveyors of music they might be, from leftfield indie rock releases, to an obscure instructional recording of how to teach your parrot to speak—in German—the record shop clerk has a wealth of eclectic and remarkable information up his/her sleeve. Whether discussing the spiralling adventure of a recent vinyl 'pick up', explaining the origins of a store name, or recalling an anecdote about the local area, the mere experience of spending extended time conversing with a record store owner has made for alarming, fascinating, hilarious, and downright weird stories of all descriptions.

At Val's Halla in Oak Park, just north of Chicago's centre, Val Callimetti, who used to work for Capitol Records in the 1960s, has now been in business for over 40 years. A real character, complete with grey afro and labrador-adorned sweater. Val is a great storyteller, and described the origin of her store's name with zeal—taken from Norse mythology, Valhalla was the "great hall of immortality in which the souls of warriors slain heroically were received by Odin and enshrined". Val's Halla, she explained, was her version of this hall—"the modest hall of mortals in which the 'soul' of music lovers seeking contentment is welcomed by experts

and fulfilled". Halla was also the name of her dog. Of some of the memorable experiences that we had, a few stood out from the rest. Joe who ran Gramophone, Chicago's internationally renowned and heavy weight house music emporium, talked of the suspicion and local politics which he struggled with around dance music in Chicago, and the lack of support for the genre due to an unfounded association with drugs and danger, despite its international reputation and musical tourism potential for the city. Jimmy, head of Forced Exposure independent distribution, which is based in Boston, warned of the threat of corporate chains, such as Best Buy, pricing out small independent stores, whilst offering us a few slick moves on the basketball court that took up part of their huge distribution warehouse. Bob Koester, 76 year-old founder of Chicago's Delmark records—America's oldest independent jazz and blues label—and owner of the amazing Jazz Record Mart, also collected old Super 8 and 16 mm film, and organised regular screenings of his collection for friends and family.

Ray, who runs Grooves on Market Street, San Francisco, used to do the light shows at the Filmore concert hall during the 1960s, so had plenty of anecdotes to recall too, but it was he who explained to us that record labels, for a period, used to issue different coloured vinyl for different genres of music: "red for rock, blue for musicals, green for world music...". These same 12" circles of colour emblazon the glass front of Ray's store—"the poor man's stained glass", he laughed: "the yellow ones are all Mormon church services... but I've covered up the labels as I don't want to scare customers off!".

At Groove Merchant up the street, owner Chris Veltri, who specialises in rare soul, funk, Brazilian (and more) told us about the recent tragedy of Sugar Pie deSanto, a celebrated soul singer from California, who had just lost her husband and all her possessions to a house fire. Groove Merchant were hosting a benefit with live bands and DJs from the local area, to try and raise some money for her. Dick, who runs Rooky Ricardo's Records across the road from Groove Merchant, also offers dance lessons, reflecting his amazing array of soul and disco 45s on sale in his store. "I mainly teach first dances for weddings now", he says. "We used to hold in-store dance parties, but we had to stop after a gun went off on the dance floor, and the police were called! Everyone ducked or ran out of the store. We hid in the cupboard and when we climbed back out, this mysterious gun was just left on the middle of the dance floor."

Top Right: Emma Pettit interviews Cornelius Harris at Underground Resistance's store, Somewhere in Detroit, Detroit, Michigan
Middle Right: Grooves Records, San Francisco, California
Bottom Right: Reckless Records, Chicago, Illinois

Top Left: Village Music, Mill Valley, California (RIP)
Middle Left: Val's Halla, Oak Park, Chicago, Illinois
Middle Bottom: Gramaphone, Chicago, Illinois

A conversation with Wade Wright, who runs Jack's Record Cellar, a historic San Francisco store that specialises in 78s and vinyl from the turn of the twentieth century onwards, led to a conversation about local filmmakers, including Kenneth Anger. It turned out Anger had once lived in a house known as the Russian Embassy on Fulton Street, and had bought it from the previous owner, Anton LeVey, who just happened to be the founder of the Church of Satan. Anger had filmed various scenes from his films inside the house, but it also turned out he had been a follower of Aleister Crowley, and lived in the house for a period with Bobby Beausoleil, was eventually connected to the Manson Family murders. Another example of the local knowledge and creative, eccentric and unexpected conversational path that you might end up taking whilst perusing the racks of 1940s dance hall waltzes.

One of my favourite encounters though, was with Larry, who runs The Thing in Brooklyn, and who we ended up visiting twice. The Thing is a thrift store based in a district called Green Point, home to a large Polish community, just up from Williamsburg, but which still feels like a comparatively 'local' neighbourhood, not yet a victim of the rapid transformation of much of New York, due to hyper-speed gentrification—something Larry was particularly articulate and passionate about. "I've noticed a change in the people walking down the street—they used to stop and say hello, and now I've become invisible." A miniature city made up of boxes and boxes of 'stuff'—one man's junk is another man's treasure as they say. From piles of books and comics, to glassware and crockery, old VHS players, pairs of shoes, rails of clothes, stacks of videos, DVDs, lampshades, picture frames and furniture (all this sitting above a chaotic yet seductive basement filled with vinyl crates, so close together you have to hold your breath to squeeze down the isles). Larry's stock is generally accumulated through visiting people selling off collections, estates, and unwanted belongings, for a host of different reasons. He told us of widows selling their husbands' suits and collections of LPs, at a loss to know what to do with years of accumulated possessions; young couples having moved into a new house, ready to transform it, but for the obstacle of 30 heavy boxes of books and records left in the attic or garage. Even crack addicts desperate for cash, who had come across an abandoned collection of vintage magazines, Larry jumping in the back of a van with them to exchange cash for stock, no questions asked, on the side of a remote stretch of freeway.

An excitable storyteller, he relished in animatedly describing his very first outing to make a collection, a response to an advert he'd placed in the local paper, which after a phone call involving heavy breathing and a man offering some magazines—"I have some things I think you'd be very interested in"—led him to a family home. Relieved that the husky voice was due to the man's unfortunate reliance on a respirator rather than the mark of a deviant, Larry was invited into the house, and subsequently offered a selection of valuable comics, rare books and a smattering of hardcore S&M porn magazines, not to mention a collection of photographs of the gentleman's daughter—who brightly showed him out once the deal was done— performing unspeakable acts on the family dog. I fear you might not learn quite the back story to that first pressing Stevie Wonder LP that you just found and bought on eBay.

What a record shop can do that online bidding and downloading can't, is bring people together. It offers more opportunities for friendship, new ideas, unexpected discoveries, chance encounters, knowledge, cultural and musical introductions, and a more visceral and emotional experience than any Internet chat room, or email, or MySpace comment, can ever really replicate. And while I don't pretend that computer technology hasn't benefited my own life in a trillion different ways, a homogeneous existence built around a screen and a keyboard, html code and a virtual information highway, doesn't quite cut it—at least not in isolation.

In relation to this, one of the most enjoyable and enlightening interviews for me, was in New York, with Jack Rabid, the editor of *Big Takeover* magazine, a bi-annual independent music magazine that has been supporting and celebrating new music for over 25 years. As well as being hugely knowledgeable in music history, Jack's reflections were compelling because of his perspective on developments in technology, and the impact that their convenience— "a dirty word", he says, has had on human interaction, particularly in connection to music:

> Progress itself is not always good. There is usually a good and a bad side to it for human beings. There is something gained and something unnecessarily lost at exactly the same time.... The bad thing is that it has isolated people more, and the need for a community in a music scene is something people feel deep seated in their souls.... The tribal aspect of human beings in modern society is something we are

Top and Bottom: Rooky Ricardo's, San Francisco, California

constantly trying to invalidate, when, in fact, it's throbbing within our breast at all times.... The natural aspect of the music scene is that you are constantly not only meeting people, but shoving up against them in a very space-invading way, at a really hot concert... and in a crowded record store, in the same way, as you're thumbing through the records, you're bumping into people, saying 'excuse me do you mind if I look at the B section?' and the next thing you know, you're talking to them, and exchanging information, and it just sucks that people are now sitting at home, alone, shopping for their records.

When we started out, one of our main inquiries for the film was into whether technology has negatively impacted the independent record store. While this is definitely the case to an extent, the question cannot really be answered in such a simplistic way. The arrival of MP3s to the market place has undoubtedly proved challenging for the independent store on the street, but we have also seen many, many examples of stores embracing these changes and developments, moving forward, reaping the benefits of online and the digital, making real successes and, as Marc Joseph, photographer and author of *New and Used* points to in a recent review of his book on second hand books and vinyl—"defiantly thriving".

It is evident that a significant number of stores have closed recently—even when we returned to New York after two months in other parts of America, one store had closed, another had moved location, and one of our final interviews left us with a very bleak prospect for the shop in question. However, it also clear that many of these stores have got a lot of life-blood left in them yet, and are ready to fight the good fight. Vinyl sales are, statistically, more healthy than ever; online sections of these businesses are being improved and are being used to support the neighbourhood shop with an international clientele, and lots of stores have plans for expansion—venues, labels, digital stores, live promoting. While music exists, and people continue to love music, the independent record store surely has a chance—the format we consume it with might change in part, but there is still a role for a store owner, tastemaker or expert, in this context, and more than that, people still love vinyl, and want to buy it, trade it, own it, play it.

And there's so much of it, it's not suddenly going to disappear, unless perhaps, it all gets recalled for use in the production of weapons, as much shellac was during the Second World War, and vinyl was subsequently introduced. The other story that emerges and perhaps offers an additional, more real threat to these businesses—unlike the ability of a record store to adapt and refine in the light of technological advancement—is the runaway train that is real estate and property value. It is this which looms darkly, reflected in the rapid gentrification of less refined areas of the American city (and beyond), from New York, to Chicago, to Boston, to Los Angeles, to San Francisco, all of which are seeing luxury apartments rise like mushrooms overnight, and in the homogenisation of local areas through the arrival of chain stores such as Starbucks, Radio City, Best Buy, our equivalent mega-supermarkets making the British headlines in the same negative light.

Not a new story, but one that is playing out with an unhappy ending. When corporate chain stores move into a local area, the property prices shoot up, pushing out long-established local businesses and the history, character, and specialist knowledge that they might offer. It is this which appears to be the other villain of the story, and might provide the final nail in the coffin for the independent record store, which is really only one example in a whole spectrum of local and individual businesses under threat from the corporate machine. Not ignoring the role creative industries have in this process of change—artists and musicians are often the first to move to an 'undeveloped' area of a city, before the media, then the hangers on, with the property developers close behind. But for the purposes of preserving independent music, and securing its role in nurturing identity, individuality and choice—support your local record shop while you can —there's a slice of cultural history disappearing. Or, as a spokesman on a BBC news report said once, "soon we'll all be living in Tesco".

Grooves, San Francisco, California

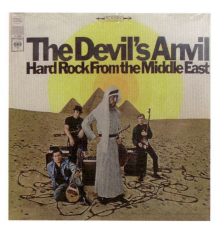

X-Ray Spex, *Germ Free Adolescents*, EMI, 1978

Cal Costa, Soundtrack, Philips, 1969

The Devil's Anvil *Hard Rock from the Middle East*, Columbia, 1967

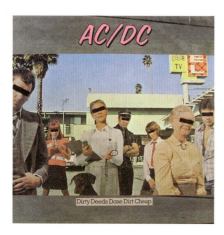

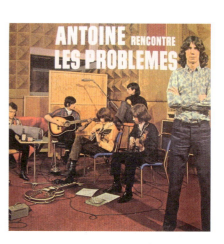

AC/DC, *Dirty Deeds Done Dirt Cheap*, Warner, 1976

Ray Swinfield, *One For Ray: The Late Night Sound of Ray Swinfield*, Morgan

Antoine et Les Problemes, *Vogue*, 1966

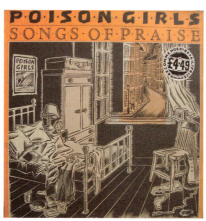

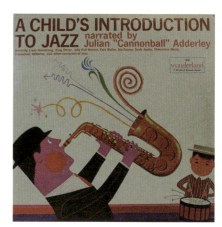

Harold McNair, Soundtrack, RCA Victor, 1968

Poison Girls, *Songs of Praise*, Xntrix, 1985

V/A, *A Child's Introduction To Jazz: Narrated By Julian 'Cannonball' Adderley*, Riverside, 1961

Oneida, *The Wedding*, Jagjaguwar, 2005

Peter Herbolzheimer, *Wide Open*, MPS, 1973

Rezillos, *Can't Stand the Rezillos*, Sire, 1978

Nausea, *Extinction*, Profane Existence, 1990

GG Allin, *Always Was, Is and Always Shall Be*, Black Orange Records, 1980

The Mops, *Psychedelic Sounds in Japan*, JVC, 1968

Various, *Las Vegas Grind* vol 6, Strip Records, 2000

Nancy Sinatra and Lee Hazlewood, *Did You Ever?*, RCA, 1971

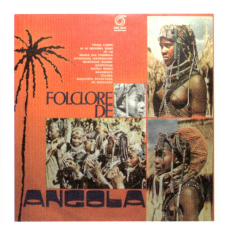

Various, *Folclore de Angola*, Roda.

A Conversation with Bill Brewster

What was the first record you ever bought?

Benny Hill's "Ernie the Fastest Milkman in the West" from Boots in Grimsby.

What are you collecting at the moment?

At the moment, I'm getting more into French music, 1970s rock and fusion stuff, and a lot of European releases of various styles. I started collecting pop 45s like most people, I guess. My first loves were David Essex and Marc Bolan and I went through a serious glam phase with a side order of Motown, followed by punk and northern soul, then post-punk stuff. A brief unsuccessful dalliance with jazz-funk led the way towards 1980s funk (bands like Spunk, Mutiny etc), hip hop, electro, diverting into 1960s girl groups and southern soul—James Carr is my God) before meeting house and retroactively going back to discover all the disco that house stole for inspiration. Since then it's been a mish mash of all of that and loads of other stuff like disco 45s, psych-rock, French chansons and Italo-disco.

Which is your favourite record store?

King Bee in Manchester is magnificent. When I lived in New York, Chelsea Book & Records (sadly no longer with us) was my weekly temple.

What is your most treasured find?

I don't really have one. It's all music, innit? My favourite record is probably David Essex's "Rock On", which I loved as a kid and I still have my original copy, all scratched up and knackered and stained with cider. But that's another one I bought from Boots in Grimsby. I've got more valuable records but I just don't classify them financially.

Name the most memorable episode set during record hunting

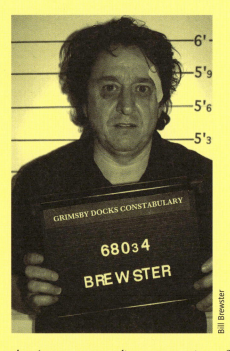

Bill Brewster

days (a store, a personality, a conversation, a find, a dodgy deal, etc).

An old friend and legend in New York called John Hall briefly owned a record store in Tribeca. I took fellow collector Dave 'Joey Negro' Lee with me one day, and after perusing the racks for an hour or so Dave picked out a few pieces he wanted to buy and handed them to John at the counter. John scratched his chin, ummed and ahhed for a few minutes then said, "Sorry I can't sell you these". He had opened the shop to sell his own (brilliant) collection but couldn't bring himself to. Needless to say it soon closed down and John ended up living in a flophouse on the Bowery. He still has his records in a storage unit, though.

How have eBay and the Internet impacted on record collecting and the local store?

It's changed how I shop, but I think that's as much to do with having small children and not being able to go out at weekends on digging trips. I do use it, but nothing beats going into a real shop. It has obviously had a huge impact on collecting, as you can tell by the hundreds of shops that have closed in the past eight years.

What is the future for the record store and vinyl?

There is a market for the record store but to survive, it either has to be competitively priced— as King Bee in Manchester, or it has to have a strong online presence. Vinyl is finished as a serious art form for new releases, though there's no reason why it won't continue as a boutique item for certain (smaller) labels. Bottom line is, I collect music—not formats—so while it's sad, there has never been a better and more accessible time for music.

Originally a chef, a football pundit and record collector, Bill began DJing in earnest and gaining a reputation for eclecticism in the late 1980s, while living in New York and running DMC's American operation. He cut his teeth playing 'Low Life' warehouse parties in Harlem and the East Village. He is also author of the definitive history of DJing, *Last Night A DJ Saved My Life.*

:::

A Conversation with Rob da Bank

:::

Do you buy records? Have you got a favourite record shop?

Yes, I spend about £150 minimum on—mostly vinyl—every week. I shop at Sounds Of The Universe, Phonica, Honest Jons, Black Market and Sister Ray from time to time. Since I've had a baby I've noticed the time I'm allowed to browse in record shops has been unfairly curtailed!

Can you remember the first album you bought?

Yes it was the Stone Roses' *Stone Roses,* and I listened to it about 400 times solidly.

Does album artwork matter? Do you have a favourite album cover / why do you like it?

I absolutely love all the 4AD sleeves that Vaughan Oliver and his V23 studio created... the Pixies dog one and Cocteau Twins swirly blue and red sleeve in particular. That man is one of the best designers ever. Obviously Peter Saville and Factory didn't do a bad job either and there are so many other great sleeves. Obviously, now that people are only

creating images to go on CDs or computers some of that magic is gone.

Is it death to vinyl and the record shop?

Well I wouldn't say total extinction, but the specialists will get more specialist and the best dance music record shops will survive, but I imagine the major chains will stop selling vinyl fairly soon. It's sad, but inevitable.

Are people missing out on something by only having MP3s and music on their computers?

Of course! I see kids of 16 now who have never owned a CD or piece of vinyl. You can't describe what it's like to only own a few pieces of vinyl growing up, that were like your mates almost— you could spend a whole night in your room with them, just looking at them and caressing them— or was that just me?!

British DJ Rob da Bank, best known for his work on BBC Radio One, also runs company Sunday Best, which includes live events, a record label and the annual festival on the Isle of Wight, Bestival.

Rob da Bank

:::

A Conversation with Chan Marshall

:::

What was the first record you ever bought?

Debbie Harry's *Koo Koo* and Hüsker Dü's *Metal Circus.*

Which is your favourite record store?

There are so many dude, that's not fair, there are so many great ones all over the globe. There's a similar 'community' vibe in vinyl shops, the owners of the stores are usually behind the counter, and can tell you this and that about all kinds of genres and different decades....

They're the real headmasters of the vinyl trade, it's much more fun to shop around a store with the owner giving you tips about certain quality of sound in opposing albums... and you can't get that online. Vinyl boutique shopping... dude. Vinyl's the only way to go. And the whole world knows that. If Apple would make a cool record player everybody would buy vinyl again.

What is your most treasured find?

A Bob Dylan bootleg vinyl from Italy.

Which is your favourite album artwork and why?

Otis Redding vinyl bootleg of my mom's. It's a photo of Otis singing live, bending over, trying to get that note out, he's wet with sweat, and you know, if you were there, from that cover photo, that he'd be singin' balls-out rad-ass loud soul perfection!!! With that smile and those dimples. Great cover. Otis was workin'!

Name the most memorable episode set during record hunting days (a store, a personality, a conversation, a find, a fight, a dodgy deal, etc).

I remember in Altanta, at Wax n Fact on Moreland Avenue, I had to get rid of everything I owned, for personal reasons, and I had to sell that aforementioned Otis Bootleg record. I knew I should have kept it, but I really needed the money. After these past eight years, I have searched and searched for that same record on vinyl. So yeah, most memorable episode—me getting rid of my favourite record, like a true idiot. So yeah, if anybody finds it, possibly at Wax n Facts in Atlanta, it should have my mom's name on it, handwritten, on the cover (Myra Russell, in cursive) please send it to me: big reward.

Has your approach towards collecting changed with the Internet?

I buy no vinyl from the Internet, because there are record shops. The only reason I don't 'collect' much of anything anymore is 'cause I am always on tour... and when I get the chance to 'collect' records, clothes, etc, it's usually in some far off place and I always return home to boxes and boxes of this and that. And yeah, I got a good selection in Athens last year from Wuxtry Records, they shipped to me. Stuff from probably many urban American's grandparents setup, Dizzy, Deitrich, old shit. That's what sucks about the Internet: I tried to download John Coltrane's *Crescent* record a couple of months ago, and guess which track wasn't included? "Lonnie's Lament"! My favourite song on *Crescent*. I didn't download the record. I am waiting to find a vinyl copy of it.

How have eBay and the Internet impacted on record collecting and the local store?

I love going into record stores in smaller cities 'cause it's always such a mish-mash of great finds, I have never shopped on the Internet for vinyl. And definitely, I would much more be inclined to download Nico's *Chelsea Girl* 'cause I never owned it on vinyl, but say, I'd much rather shop for Elvis Costello's *This Year's Model*, 'cause I owned it on vinyl and know the quality of sound. In a perfect world, if I could actually find a copy of

Nico's *Chelsea Girl* in a record store, then I'd buy it, but I can't find it when I'm 'casually' hunting. We need the Internet and we also need vinyl. It's so much fun to go into a record shop. Kids don't know about that 'rush'.

What is the future for the record store and vinyl?

Well I'm no fortune teller, but I think the smaller record shops will maintain and continue, and that the giant CD megastores may perish. Vinyl can always have an audience, the sooner we educate our nieces and nephews and kids about the importance of music history.

That being said, they can learn the importance of sound quality. With them actually sitting down with an album, re-learning how they actually listen to music. The importance of 'message' within music from the past, is completely foreign to kids today. Civil rights, class system, political issues, immigrant stories, etc. Music from the past told all those truths of temperature during all those years of vinyl records.

The downloadable world is a market driven toward modern music, pop sensation of the week. Every label and their grandma are trying to absorb the human mind's eye when people hit the Internet, to sell the new releases.

The whole thing about record stores, vinyl shops, is that a kid can go in and learn about music history. With the Internet, it's all pitched for a musical 'now' and 'next'. Kids need that music education. It's part of our world's history. It tells the story of us. Downloading can get only get stronger, but I think record companies should definitely think up new ideas to get the kids of today interested in the music of yesterday. 'Cause the downloading situation wouldn't be in the power position it's in without the history of blues, jazz, country, folk, soul, r & b and rock 'n' roll. It's all that music that created all these fans, which created all these record stores.

Dude.
I'm on both sides.
Anything for the kids' minds.
'Cause it's music that set me free, that's for certain.

Cat Power is the stage name of American singer/ songwriter Chan Marshall, whose most recent album *Jukebox* was released on Matador Records earlier this year.

Chan Marshall

Olly Dixon and Tim Lawton (together the Filthy Dukes)

OLLY DIXON

My brother used to take me to a Winchester car boot sale on a Sunday and we would spend hours looking through piles of old vinyl. I didn't know what I was looking for and was far more interested in the cover art; I think I still am. The dimensions of vinyl are amazing and some artwork is simply outrageous. One week my brother forced me to spend most of my pocket money on a copy of Johnny Cash *Live at San Quentin*; 50p seemed a lot for some old country singer none of my friends had heard of. Around this time I also had an *Almost Famous* moment. At the start of the film William Miller's older sister, who is running away from home to become an air hostess, leaves him a bag full of records under his bed. She says "one day you will be cool, look under your bed. It'll set you free." My sister was living in London and I was much younger and light-years from cool. I found a box of her records in the loft; The Doors, Rolling Stones, Beatles, Jethro Tull, Carol King, Jimi Hendrix. I'm not sure they made me cool but it opened a whole new world to me, not only music, but fashion, art, attitude, everything seemed more interesting all of a sudden. From this point, I was obsessed with buying old vinyl, I don't think I ever went looking for specific records; it was always more a case of chance. Either I loved the cover, or recognised the name of a producer or label, or remembered a name from an interview or article. Everything from Bauhaus to BBC Radiophonic Workshop, Blood Sweet & Tears to Krystof Komeda, Led Zeppelin to Pascal Roge. Eventually I started DJing and playing my scratchy old records at parties. I played "A Boy Named Sue" from the *Live at San Quentin Album* at a *Dazed* party and Bjork got up and danced—50p well spent!!

Olly Dixon is one part of London-based DJ and producer collective Filthy Dukes, who are currently recording their debut album for Polydor. He also runs the influential club night Kill 'Em All, which has residencies at Fabric and the Bar Fly, and works regularly with the Adventures in the Beetroot Field group of independent promoters.

TIM NOAKES

One day my mum took me shopping to Woolworths and told me that I could choose a present to keep me occupied while she held a Tupperware party. Being 1982, and the fact that I was four years old, we immediately veered off towards the toy section to enlist another GI Joe recruit for my gang of plastic mercenaries. But we never made it. On the way there, something happened. For some reason, my eyes locked onto a big eye that was staring out of the blackness of a 7" record sleeve; Steve Miller's *Abracadabra*. Intrigued and slightly unnerved, I told my mum that war could wait and I wanted that as my present. All afternoon while a room of women compared microwaveable dishes and picnic plates, I sat at our record player listening to the single over and over again, peering into the eye and repeating, "Abra-abra-cadabra, I'm going to reach out and grab ya..." Whatever this voodoo was, I liked it.

In the 25 years since Miller cast his spell over my ears, vinyl's black magic has yet to wear off. Well, I don't listen to *Abracadabra* much anymore, but that trip to Woolworths marked the start of a journey into sound that has made me who I am today—a music freak.

The pursuit of new and rare grooves has taken me on many musical tangents over the intervening decades—from British hair metal and East Coast hip-hop, to French electro and Congolese kwassa kwassa. This never ending search has meant that whatever city I come across, I'll always be sure to get my fingers dirty searching through dusty crates for that elusive instrumental version of Dr Dre's *The Chronic*, or the original dub plate pressing of Jennifer Lara's "I Am in Love". There's just something magical about walking into a record store and not knowing what you're going to come out with, whether that's Rob's Records in Nottingham, House of Records in Santa Monica, Fat Beats in NYC, or Gordo & Celio's in Sao Paulo. That feeling will stay with me until the day I die, or, God forbid, the day record stores die.

Do you know the worst thing about collecting records? I'm plagued with guilt that I'll never have time to listen to them all. Still, I suppose I can look at the covers. RIP Scorpion Records, High Wycombe, 1977–2006.

Tim Noakes is music editor of Britain's *Dazed and Confused* magazine.

Rooky Ricardo's, San Francisco, California

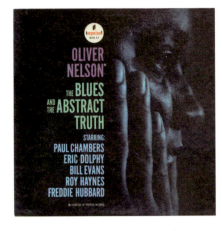

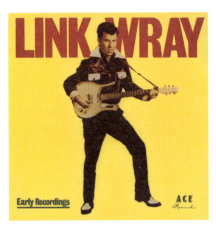

Oliver Nelson, *The Blues and the Abstract Truth*, Impulse!, 1961

Link Wray, *Link Wray Early Recordings*, Rollercoaster/ Ace, 1963

Tubby Hayes & Paul Gonsalves All Stars, *Chance of Setting*. WRC

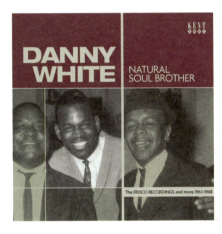

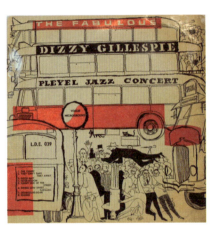

Danny White, *Natural Soul Brother/One Way Love Affair*, SSS International, 1968

Dizzy Gillespie, *Pleyel Jazz Concert*, Vogue, 1953

Ima Costa, *Folclore de Cabo Verde*, Osiris

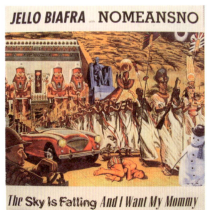

The Rolling Stones, *Mother's Little Helper*, Decca, 1966

Jello Biafra and NoMeansNo, *The Sky is Falling and I Want My Mommy*, Alternative Tentacles, 1991

Frank Cunimondo Trio, *Introducing Lynn Marino*, Mondo

Pharoah Sanders Quintet, *Pharoah's First*, ESP, 1965

Independencia, *Voz de Cabo Verde*, Voz de Cabo Verde

Question Mark, *Be Nice To The People*, Shadoks, 1974

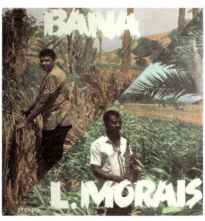

Dizzy Gillespie and His Orchestra Featuring Chano Pozo, Vogue

Bana and L Morais, *Soundtrack*, Vos de Cabo Verde

Devo, *Duty Now For The Future*, Warner Bros, 1979

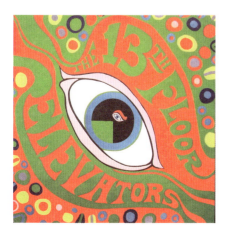

13th Floor Elevators, *Psychedelic Sound Of...*, International Artists, 1967

The Deirdre Wilson Tabac Soundtrack, RCA, 1970

Marconi Nataro, *No Sub Reino dos Metazoarios*, Timelag, 1973/2007

GIVE ME YOUR ZONOPHONE NUMBER

Bob Stanley

When you feel some affinity with a man in Crouch End crushed to death by the weight of newspapers he'd accumulated over the years, it's good to have Walter Benjamin in your corner. The philosopher once said that the collector has "taken up arms against dispersal. The great collector is touched to the core by the confusion and dispersal in which things are found in this world." Turning anarchy into order. With a little help from PVC sleeves and wooden Schweppes crates, that's what I've been doing for the best part of four decades.

I'm glad Walter has legitimised it for me and I feel less like a sociopath, and more than one step removed from the Unabomber. Besides, I've been plagued with doubt over the last couple of years as to whether a lifelong passion for collecting records is that different to stamp collecting. While I kind of admire the Australian woman who is now in prison for siphoning funds to feed to her Elvis habit, the advent of iTunes—with anything in my collection, and other people's, there at the click of a button—has me questioning the relevance of a rare record collection. Shouldn't it have been about the music all along? Hasn't the computer sorted out the confusion and dispersal for us?

On top of that, the stores I took for granted, the damp cellars I took pleasure in discovering, are fast disappearing. Between 2004 and 2006, a quarter of independent record shops

in Britain closed down, and it's only going to get worse. EBay, Musicstack, Netsounds and Gemm have negated the need for retail space. The idea of pulling into a small town and checking out the second hand record shop is now more of a lucky break than the norm. And in this way, the collector's habit of a lifetime has changed from an hour or so rummaging through crates for one piece of gold, to clicking a button and waiting a week for it to arrive in the post. No checking the label credits, running your finger over that dubious hairline scratch, nothing tactile. The thrill, as Clydie King sang, has gone.

Still, it's a hard habit to break. The means of locating them may have changed for the worse, but there's still so much to discover beyond the scraped-clean boxes marked 'psych', 'northern' and 'punk'. Start to explore DIY, soft pop, glam, bubblegum, plus whatever pigeonhole fits my favourite avant-pop eccentric, Stavely Makepeace, and you'll realise these genres still have plenty of mileage for the thrill seeker. Just the sight of an obscure British label from the 1970s like Sticky, Bumble, or Concord can cause a slight quickening of my pulse, as Aladdin, Flair, End and Gone did for doo wop collectors, some of pop's earliest archivists back in the 1960s. And if I am lucky enough to find a box of records in a junk shop there's always the chance of coming across 5" 78s of children's music, promotional flexis for Esso Blue, cereal packet records by the Monkees... or, best of all, acetates—the

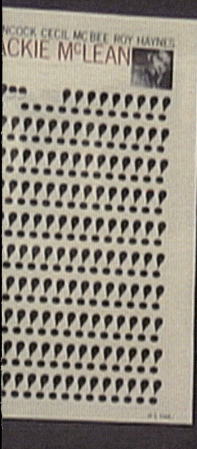

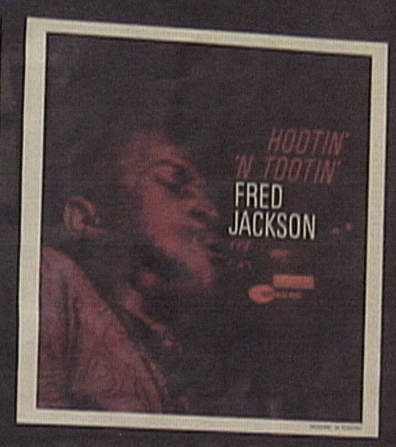

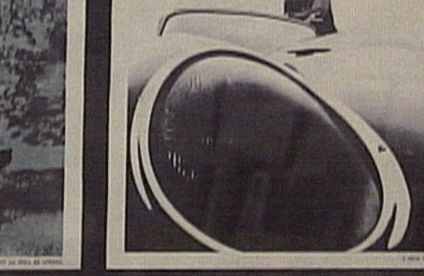

strange, one-off pressings that retain their new, weirdly electrical smell indefinitely. Records. In all shapes and sizes. They're wonderful.

I can't say that I grew up surrounded by music. My dad was, and remains, a hi-fi buff searching for music to match up to his record deck. There was plenty of Wagner but—*Bridge Over Troubled Water* aside—not much pop. It hadn't always been this way. Before they married at 19 and abandoned fripperies like 45s, mum and dad had made a tidy collection of rock 'n' roll instrumentals and trad jazz EPs. What's more, they didn't seem to care about them anymore and let me toy with them.

Aping my dad's audiophile tendencies, I handled them with what I thought was great care. They seemed mysterious and important. The coloured labels had me hooked: Elmer Bernstein's *Staccato's Theme* on purple Capitol with that crazy tower; Sandy Nelson's *Teen Beat* on red-and-white Top Rank with the naked gong beater; Duane Eddy's *Because They're Young* on black-and-silver London which somehow looked the most important. My favourite—a tell-tale sign in retrospect—was the Shadows' *FBI* on a white Columbia label with a big red 'A' across it. As I learnt to read, the label details fascinated me. Who or what was "Gormley" and why was the word written in brackets underneath *FBI*? At some point I must have been able to read "Demonstration copy not for sale". My head was turned before I was even at primary school.

Whenever I got dragged round to Auntie Pam's or Uncle Mick's, the surest way of shutting me up was to leave me alone with a box of records. If I was lucky, the amused family friend would let me keep one. This is how the Small Faces' "I Can't Make It", with a boxed Decca label, came my way, though I much preferred the novelty b-side "Just Passing". One rocker 'uncle' had a record room, which is etched in my mind as though it were the Sistine Chapel. On the wall, in what I assumed for years was an example of false memory syndrome, were a row of Coral labels with no records attached. I was in my 30s before I saw another set—apparently they were produced by the Decca group for record store decoration. My 'rocker uncle' was a villainous type, who no doubt attained his ultra-rare set by brandishing a flick knife at the throat of a bryll-creemed shop assistant, but I wasn't about to blow the whistle. 'Rocker uncle' gave me a copy of *With the Beatles*, my very first long player.

Few kids are fortunate enough to have grandparents who not only live by the seaside but also run a sweet shop. If this wasn't luck enough, Nana also fed my collection by picking up 45s from a junk shop round the corner. She would then make sleeves for them by cutting a hole in the centre of a candy-striped sweet bag. Favourites included the highly appropriate "Sticky Sticky" by the 1910 Fruitgum Company (flip to the American hit "123 Red Light") on a yellow Pye International demo, and "Groovin' With Mr Bloe" on DJM, which has rarely left my side since.

I was nine before I had pocket money and could add to the collection of my own volition. Sparks' *Amateur Hour*, on the intriguingly colourful Island label in a plain pink bag, became the first of several thousand. Buying records as a kid didn't necessarily involve going into a record shop, which always felt like quite an adult move. In Brief Encounter, Celia Johnson goes to Boots to buy a book to read on the train and, likewise, Surrey Cameras in Purley stocked records until the 1980s. This diversity wasn't unusual. Newsagents would sell ex-jukebox singles, placed on carousels as if they were birthday cards, at bargain prices. The singles were re-sleeved by companies like Star Hits, with their K-Tel wannabe purple and orange graphics, who obtained the stock from pubs; they were often fairly beaten up and always with a plastic spider centre rather than the original. A newsagents on Russell Hill Road, Purley, was where I discovered the Beach Boys' wonderful *Sail On Sailor* on the Reprise label, steamboat and all. Most Star Hits fare was less glamorous.

There was always Woolworths, who even now have the hits placed on the wall according to their chart position. The branch in Redhill, Surrey, was where I bought Amateur Hour; in my teens, Woolies produced the best value for money, as whenever a record would drop out of the Top 75 it switched instantly to the half-price basket on the counter. Second-guessing these bargains before Tuesday lunchtime, when the new chart was announced, was a minor art form. Generally, the more cultish the group, the easier this was to work out— wait for a number one and it could take months but the likes of Echo & The Bunnymen, The Teardrop Explodes and New Order were a piece of cake.

The 'real' shops tended to be run by more serious looking types. They would always be playing Joni Mitchell, or someone who sounded just like her, and always albums rather than singles. Redhill, where I lived until I was 14, had two independent record shops alongside Woolies. One was L&H Cloake's, housed in a post-war shopping parade south of the football ground. Here I made my first album purchase: *More*

Hot Butter, on the blue Pye International label and reduced to 50p, was loaded with early Moog novelties that tickled my ten-year old palate. It was followed soon after by *The World Of The Tornados* on Decca—more instrumentals, and the beginning of a lifelong obsession with Joe Meek productions. Cloake's had a more impressive Croydon branch arranged over two floors that still had wood-lined listening booths upstairs. Even in the 1970s these seemed like an intriguing relic, and only classical customers were allowed to use them.

The other outlet in Redhill was Rhythm, on the corner of a Victorian arcade, which had a jaunty, 1950s sign of crooked letters. They sold singles at 59p—cheaper than anywhere else, not because they were trying to undercut WH Smith (75p at that point) but probably because they were too relaxed to noticed their competitors' pricing policy. It was the archetypal, family run record shop and—though no one knew it in the mid-1970s—living on borrowed time.

Aged 13, on a shopping trip to Croydon, I discovered Beano's. In all honesty, it was one of the half dozen most significant moments in my life. Beano's proclaimed itself to be the biggest second hand record shop in Britain, and—though it now survives in reduced circumstances—after 30 years of criss-crossing the nation, I have little doubt that it was. My portal to music from the past was Jimmy Savile's *Old Record Record*, a two-hour Sunday lunchtime show on Radio One that played entire Top Tens, plus 30 minutes of lesser hits, from that day in history. Discovering Beano's meant that, after hearing them for the first time, I could actually buy Keith West's *Excerpt From A Teenage Opera*, Traffic's *Hole In My Shoe*, or Dick And Deedee's *The Mountain's High*, and all on the original labels rather than ugly re-issues. At 15, I got a Saturday job selling cheese, eggs and bacon. It was two doors along from Beano's.

The money that didn't go directly from Croydon's cheese-crazy public to Beano's went to Bonaparte's. This was the hip local store, the one you'd go to for 'underground' records, and I made it my destination of choice once I discovered the Independent Chart in *Smash Hits*. Always a fiend for listings, this alternative to the regular Top 30 threw up all manner of exotic new names (Joy Division, Cabaret Voltaire, Fire Engines, all very important sounding to an impressionable 15-year old) and a wild array of brand new labels; Manchester had Factory, Liverpool had Zoo and Inevitable, 4AD were from somewhere dark and misty (turned out to be Wandsworth), even East Anglia had Backs.

Behind the Bonaparte's counter was a guy with pinprick eyes, a baggy jumper, very red hair and very white skin. He couldn't have got work anywhere else. This is the shop where I bought the Beatles albums (as opposed to the red and blue compilations), *The Fall*, *Love's Da Capo* and *Forever Changes*, all the Postcard 45s (which had the best packaging of the era), and innumerable early 1980s 7"s. Chart records I tended to buy in Allders department store, a subconscious decision to try and keep some cred with the skinny kid in Bonaparte's. Once he was playing something that sounded like a minor Factory group, all drum machine, Martin Hannett reverbs and East Lancs melancholy. I asked the kid who it was. He replied: "Errr... me!".

This was the exact difference between Bonaparte's (plus big brothers like Rough Trade and Eastern Bloc) and Our Price. A branch of the latter had opened up a few doors along from Bonaparte's, in a poky Victorian shed adjacent to East Croydon train station. As it sold mostly cassettes it never really meant much to me. But it was a stonewall certainty that none of the staff ever got to play their Soundhog demos alongside the cassettes on EMI and CBS. I managed to collect a good number of the more obscure Factory releases (Section 25, The Names, Minny Pops) from Bonaparte's. All would have been too marginal for the slick and soul-less Our Price. The problem was, I wanted to work in a record shop and neither Beano's nor Bonaparte's were advertising.

In 1984, I started work in the Epsom branch of Our Price, which had by then become the second largest record retailer in Britain after Woolworths. Our Price's mentality was based on non-browsing. I'd always thought of Rhythm and Cloake's in Redhill as somewhere to hang out, kill time, and gaze at the Beat Merchants compilation of 1960s bands—wondering why I'd never heard of any of them and what it could all be about. It operated as good book stores still do; somewhere to escape from the rain, wait for a lift, think about what you might do with your next spare fiver.

Entering any branch of Our Price you would certainly be blinded by the light, but you were less likely to be revved up like a deuce. Aesthetics didn't come into it. The idea was that you'd be drawn through the aisles via shrieking fluorescents to the counter at the back, which was raised to make even the most Velma or Shaggy-like member of staff seem like a tower of resourcefulness and catalogue proficiency. The company's boss—who's name escapes me but, trust me, he looked exactly like the image in your mind—was irritatingly

Top Left: David Lashmar outside of Beano's, Croydon
Middle Left: Sounds of the Universe, London
Bottom Left: Honest Jons, London

Top Right: Vinyl Junkies, London
Middle Right: Vinyl Junkies, London
Bottom Right: Vinyl Junkies, London

accurate in his five-year forecast that he could shut down every other high street record shop in Britain.

Local stores had been sitting back, doing little beyond waiting for customers to walk in and ask for number two, number six, and that weird electronic thing at number 16 ("that'll be Pepper Box by The Peppers, sir"). Our Price looked like Dixons. Which wasn't a good thing. Everything was red and white and clean and bright, and nobody there was going to snigger if you couldn't pronounce *Amoureuse* by Kiki Dee properly. Independents fell like bowling pins. Even Bonaparte's.

The singular change between the likes of Cloake's, Rhythm, and Bonaparte's, and the advent of Our Price was that you were far less likely to walk in and hear a song you'd never heard before. Therefore, you wouldn't buy the unheard song, take it home, impress your friends, and pass on the joy. Instead,it seemed Phil Collins would be number one forever. Soon, Virgin and HMV joined in the process of blandification; Madonna's *Material Girl* seemed to sum up the whole miserable changeover, especially when one in three customers bought the bloody thing in March 1985.

In catering to the mundane and eliminating the mystery of the unknown, these new chains had set themselves up to be shut down by the digital revolution. It's a neat irony that the specialist shops were the only ones equipped to survive. It's hard to feel much sympathy. The smartest kid on the block turned out to be the Our Price founder who floated the company in 1984 and sold out to WH Smith two years later. Maybe he didn't trust the feel of a compact disc, felt it wasn't built to last. He had a point.

Until recently a CD copy of Dennis Wilson's *Pacific Ocean Blue* would regularly fetch triple figures on eBay. Released in the early 1990s, it wasn't well mastered; like a lot of early Sony CDs, it contained an extraordinary amount of background noise (Laura Nyro's *New York Tendaberry* took this to extremes with a high-pitched noise throughout the quiet piano passages that would drive under 25s, I'm reliably informed, to vacate the room quietly and quickly). It also came without sleevenotes, in an unsightly red 'jewel case', the cumbersome encasing that was adopted without question early on by CD manufacturers. While CDs were supposedly indestructible, customers soon discovered the cases would scratch and crack within seconds of purchase.

The re-issue of *Pacific Ocean Blue* was for a different generation, for a discerning buyer who knew that the CD was a dying format. It included all the relevant bonus tracks and didn't sound as if you were listening to it directly under the Gatwick flypath. Once it was issued, nobody wanted or needed the original. Its value plummeted to nothing overnight. An original vinyl copy, on the other hand, only became more desirable.

Vinyl has undoubtedly become the pop format. The vinyl boom, from the mid-1950s to the early 90s, coincided with a period that can safely be defined as pop's golden era. Nik Cohn argues that every new wave, each rebellious generation since the birth of rock in the 1950s, has been a ripple from the centre of the lake. The ripples get smaller each time, he argues. It's a valid point. That ripples such as Britpop, electroclash and new rave will be preserved for posterity primarily on CD rather than vinyl, does the format little favour. The CD—the last physical format before downloads made them irrelevent—is likely to be seen by pop historians as nothing more aesthetically pleasing than a floppy disc, little more than a way of storing information.

For an archivist—record obsessive with autistic tendencies if you're feeling less generous—the logical reaction to this lack of a future format is to turn back, dig even deeper into the history of recorded music and find out exactly why every Decca label featured a giant ear with "FFRR" printed alongside it. As well as scouring books on the early history of records, I've lately spent some time poring over a CD box set of music hall, Bear Family's thorough and highly entertaining *Round the Town*. This box has become a launching pad for my backwards lurch into pre-rock 'n' roll music, some even pre-Great War. And a little research has thrown up a whole new bunch of names to add to my list of pop heroes.

The Bee Gees showed their admiration for the inventor of recorded sound, cooing "Edison's here to stay" on their 1969 Odessa album. Although it was a French absinthe drinker by the name of Charles Cros who first realised that sound waves could be retained by means of "a delicate stylus" tracing them over lampblacked glass, it was Thomas Edison who produced the first cylinder machine in 1877, naming it the 'phonograph'—an approximation of the Greek for 'sound writing'.

So, the first format for recorded sound was a tinfoil sheet wrapped around a grooved cylinder—the sound was recorded

45

as indentations in the foil. Edison's early patents show how he had contemplated the idea of using a spiral of grooves on a flat disc, but decided to concentrate on the cylinder format. Music didn't enter the equation for Edison as his tinfoil cylinders sounded thin and quiet, so he marketed the phonograph as a way of playing back speech, mainly with stenographers in mind. Having invented the first record player, he got itchy feet and moved on to perfecting electric light, a wheeze which would bring him even more fame and wealth.

The white heat of technology forged fierce rivalries in the late nineteenth century, which led to the dawn of the record label. Patents meant everything. Edison's patent said that the sound was "embossed" onto the cylinder. At the Volta Laboratories in Washington DC, one Chichester Bell began working in 1881 with his famous cousin Alexander Graham Bell, and associate Charles Tainter, on improving Edison's phonograph. This they did by 'engraving' the cylinder and then coating it in wax. According to Louis Barfe's history of the record industry, *Where Have All The Good Times Gone*, Tainter was driven onwards by a rather British passion. His assistant Fred Gaisberg remembers Tainter as "a confirmed tea drinker...

> Indeed he taught me how to brew and enjoy it. Between the cups he would adjust the angle of the cutting stylus. In his clear Yorkshire voice he would test them with 'Caesar, Caesar, can you hear what I say?'. The stress was always laid on the sibilants, these being the most difficult sounds to record. In playing back the tests, at the slightest indication of the 's' sound, he would smile with joy and treat himself with another cup.

The crucial difference between Tainter and Bell's hand-cranked 'graphophone' and Edison's phonograph was the leap forward in sound quality, which was now good enough to record music. The Edison and Bell factions would work together in a niggly partnership for the next 40 years, with just the occasional threat of legal action against one another.

A civil war veteran and old associate of Edison called Colonel George Gouraud was sent to Europe to flog the new technology in 1888. Gouraud settled in a house on Beulah Hill, Upper Norwood, north of Croydon. It was named Little Menlo in homage to Menlo Park, New Jersey, the site of Edison's original laboratory.

Little Menlo also doubled up as a showroom for Edison's technological greatness—Gouraud's boots and windows were cleaned and his carpets brushed by electricity; when you opened a door the lights came on; and he rode the hilly terrain of Upper Norwood on his electric tricycle. Most importantly, he had a direct telephone connection to the nearby Crystal Palace and, with one of the very first Edison 'Improved Phonographs' at his disposal, this enabled him to record the venue's concerts. A recording Gouraud made in 1888 of Handel's *Israel In Egypt* still exists and is regarded as the oldest 'record' in the world. To bring the story full circle, you can now hear the recording at http://en.wikipedia.org/wiki/Israel_in_Egypt. It sounds rather like *Orchestral Manoeuvres In The Dark*—with or without the emphasis.

Wax cylinders are not, most would agree, as aesthetically pleasing as a flat disc with a label in its centre. In the same year as Gouraud's recording, Emile Berliner invented a simpler way to record sound laterally rather than vertically, onto discs. The 'gramophone' made its public debut at Philadelphia's Franklin Institute on 16 May 1888, with a rendition of "Twinkle Twinkle Little Star" in Berliner's heavy German accent. Gramophone recordings were made on zinc discs covered in a thin layer of fat, as wax would have breached Edison's copyright.

While gramophone recordings were far 'louder' than cylinders they could only be used for playback purposes, so it was in Berliner's interests to record some music professionally and flog it. Up until this point, only a Washington-based company called Columbia had been producing cylinders for entertainment; since 1889, they had scored their biggest successes with black-face singer George Johnson's *The Whistling Coon* and Len Spencer's comedy effort *Clancy's Prize Waltz Contest*. Columbia's talent scout—the music industry's first A&R man—was none other than Fred Gaisberg, Charles Tainter's erstwhile tea drinking buddy. However, without means of reproduction, each cylinder Columbia sold had to be a unique performance.

Berliner's step forward was in creating 'masters' which could be used to press up multiple copies. He poached Gaisner from Columbia, who brought his stable of acts with him. They first tried manufacturing gramophone records on a hard rubber called 'vulcanite' but, in 1897, settled on a formula used to makebuttons; this was an unholy sounding mixture of shellac (a substance obtained from the secretion of a southeast Asian beetle), cotton compound, powdered slate, and wax lubricant. Shellac was brittle as hell, but Gaisner had hit upon the

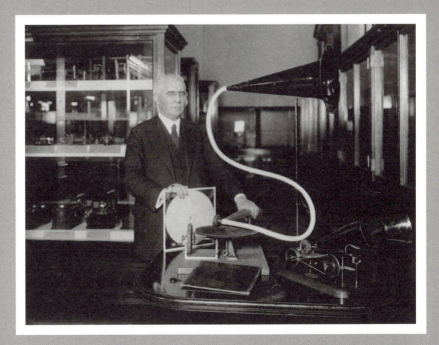

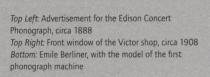

Top Left: Advertisement for the Edison Concert
Phonograph, circa 1888
Top Right: Front window of the Victor shop, circa 1908
Bottom: Emile Berliner, with the model of the first
phonograph machine

pre-eminent record format that would survive until as late as the 1960s

Berliner now moved fast and sent his enthusiastic assistant William Owen to London to make inroads into the European market. Given carte blanche, Owen started Britain's first record label—which he named rather flatly the Gramophone Company—in an office on Maiden Lane, just off of the Strand. At first he was only selling imported records, but Gaisberg joined him in mid-1898 to set up a studio in the Maiden Lane basement. His first British signing was Syria Lamonte, who also happened to be a waitress at Rules, the restaurant adjacent to the Gramophone Company's studio. More significantly, Gaisberg had struck up a friendship with portly Music Hall star Burt Shepard while sailing over from America. This gave him a direct link to the acts whose mix of comedy, bawdy innuendo, and tear-jerking sentimentality made them the biggest British pop stars of the era.

When Gaisberg met Shephard, very little music hall had been recorded—just a few cuts by Charles Coborn and Albert Chevalier made for demonstration purposes. Shellac discs could handle around three minutes of music, then (as now) the duration of your average pop song. It was a marriage made in heaven. Gaisberg cut so many records by Shephard that the star had to use a variety of pseudonyms. As Harry Taylor he cut "Has Anybody Seen Our Cat" which features the spoken introduction "Made for the Gramophone & Typewriter Company, Limited, London", read out at the kind of pace now associated with drug companies warning you about potential side effects. Pretty soon, "G&T" had a hold on many of music hall's biggest names, from Dan Leno to Florrie Forde.

One of Berliner's engineers, Eldridge Johnson, had made his name by designing a clockwork spring-wound motor to replace hand-cranking. Johnson deserves canonisation—he was also the man who invented record 'labels'. In a bid to create more eye-catching stock, he affixed paper labels to the large, unused space in the centre of the record, which had previously been simply engraved with the title. In no time, logos and bright colours were employed to create the most attractive gramophone records. One of the finest graced Berliner and Johnson's newly founded Victor label, named in 1901 after an extended legal battle. Back in Britain, William Owen had bought a painting—depicting a dog called Nipper looking curiously at a gramophone horn—entitled *His Master's Voice*. The image crossed the ocean to become Victor's logo in 1901, while the original had pride of place in Owen's office. At the start of the twentieth century there were three major American record companies: Edison, offspring of the music industry's godfather, who would only produce cylinders until 1908; the cylinder and 78-producing Columbia; and Victor, with the Gramophone & Typewriter Company its powerful British arm. If EMI and Warner ever get their threatened merger together, we'll be in pretty much the same position in the early twenty-first century. 'Independent' labels did exist and, similarly to their modern counterparts, were inclined to be swallowed up by the larger companies. Rena, a British label set up by Louis Sterling in 1908, became the first to issue double-sided discs, thus inventing the B-side (although its motto claimed "every record a picked one", as if they would never dream of including inferior recordings on the flip). Rena boomed—and was swallowed by Columbia within a year.

As patents expired, other familiar names appeared on the scene—Regal, Parlophone, Zonophone—and by 1916 there were almost 50 labels in America. In Britain, the Gramophone & Typewriter Company had ditched their cumbersome name in 1908, exchanging it for the title of the painting hanging on their office wall (and the logo they'd lent their American partner) His Master's Voice (HMV). They made it through the First World War thanks to the fashion for lump-in-the-throat patriotic songs ("It's A Long Way To Tipperary" was the first hit of its kind in 1914, starting an ignoble tradition that continued with "We'll Meet Again", "Ballad of the Green Berets", and Oleta Adams' "Get Here"). The war also ushered in the second great wave of pop, spreading from the unlikely epicentre of New Orleans. The class system had been broken by the conflict, which had brought American entertainers and soldiers over in quantity, and the new rebellious spirit of Britain was embodied in jazz music.

This soup of ragtime, blues, and marching band music made its recording debut on 26 February 1917 when the Original Dixieland Jass Band recorded "Livery Stable Blues" and "Dixie Jass Band One-Step" at Victor Studios in New York City. HMV turned down the single for British release, and—when the band played the first ever jazz show in Britain at the Hammersmith Palais in Spring 1919—Columbia pounced. Like rock 'n' roll, punk and acid house generations later, everyone leapt on the craze; the chastened HMV took out a rather desperate ad in *Talking Machine News* proclaiming "new records... suitable for JAZZING" which included a few by the Coldstream Guards. Quicker on the uptake were music hall acts, though the bright

young things digging the new breed weren't most likely to be found in the halls. *I Went A Jazzing* by Jack Pleasants appeared on Zonophone in June, and tells about meeting a girl "at the big 'Jazz Tea' at the Piccadilly Palace.... We started jazzing and when we were out of breath, she said 'Kiddo, I'm the widow of the man who jazzed himself to death'".

In America, the trail-blazing Original Dixieland Jass Band— the Bill Haley & The Comets of their day—were soon superseded by new names on new labels. Among the most significant were Vocalion, Brunswick, OKeh (who sold 70,000 copies of *Crazy Blues* by Mamie Smith's Jazz Hounds in 1920, the first crossover 'race' hit) and Paramount who specialised in blues singers including Ma Rainey, Blind Lemon Jefferson, Blind Blake, Skip James, Charley Patton and Son House.

If jazz was decidedly urban music, spawning dance crazes like The Charleston and Black Bottom, the newly defined hillbilly music (christened, like race music, by Mamie Smith's talent scout Ralph Peer) was selling like hotcakes in rural America. A Texan named Marion Try Slaughter, who took the stage name Vernon Dalhart after two neighbouring towns in the Lone Star state, had the first million seller of the genre that would become country with "The Prisoner's Song" in 1925. A year later, Variety noted that "the talking machine to the hillbilly is more practical than his bible". Classical purist Edison, who still had A&R control over every record he released in spite of increasing deafness, forgot his snobbery when it came to his money-spinning Dalhart releases.

The jazz era coincided with the birth of radio whose vacuum tubes and dynamic speakers meant that, for the very first time, the listener had volume control. The radio craze knocked record sales for a while: Victor rode out the downturn by allying themselves with the Radio Corporation of America, or RCA. What saved the bacon of the record industry was the advent of electronic recording, which followed in 1925. Until this time, recording techniques had improved little since Fred Gaisner set up the wood-lined Maiden Lane studio—musicians and singers would have to be as loud as possible, gathering in a semi-circle, with the sound sucked into a huge recording horn. Microphones and amplifiers transformed recorded sound to such an extent that the revolution wasn't announced to the public until 1927, 18 months after it happened, lest record companies' sizeable back catalogues of acoustic recordings were wiped out overnight by electrified music lovers.

The microphone also meant that lung power was no longer the be-all-and-end-all for recording singers. Rudy Vallee made his name in the late 1920s on the Victor and Velvet Tone labels with a smooth style that would have been almost inaudible in the acoustic recording era. Soon after, the singer with Paul Whiteman's band, Bing Crosby, had solo hits on Brunswick and the 'crooner' was born.

The Wall Street crash of 1929 was the next cause of music industry hand-wringing. Manufacturing of record players virtually ground to a halt in 1930. The biggest loser was Edison who, 52 years after inventing recorded sound, bowed out of the business. Incredibly, he'd been producing cylinders to the last, which can't have helped his cause in the midst of a worldwide recession. In Britain, the two biggest companies, HMV and Columbia, amalgamated to form Electric & Musical Industries Ltd (EMI) in 1931. The head office, factory, and research laboratories moved to Hayes, Middlesex, a legend that remained prominent on Beatles album sleeves more than 30 years later. At the same time, a large, purpose-built studio opened on Abbey Road, St John's Wood. For Fred Gaisberg, still in HMV's employ, it must have seemed an almighty step on from the tea-fuelled cylinder sessions of 1881.

EMI might have had the field to themselves in the 1930s, if it wasn't for Edward Lewis's nascent Decca label. Lewis had the pioneering instincts of a Spector, Oldham or McLaren. Radio stations on the continent were beaming signals over to Britain, challenging the monopoly of the staid BBC; Lewis illegally bought air-time on Radio Paris, guaranteeing Decca records an audience. He then pulled off a coup, pinching the hugely successful Jack Hylton dance band from HMV by promising its sly leader 40,000 shares in Decca, to be deposited in his Panama-registered holding company. Lewis was all about pop, dance bands, novelties, and little cared-for classical music. He may have later banned the Rolling Stones' *Beggars Banquet* sleeve for its toilet humour, but in the 1930s he was the British music industry's bad boy.

Decca also found itself at the forefront of technical innovation when war broke out in 1939, by developing full frequency range recording (FFRR) which used smaller grooves to achieve a much broader range of soundwaves than shellac could ever manage. Though it was devised to help RAF coastal command to distinguish between British submarines and German u-boats, FFRR was soon being utilised on Decca records by pianist Charlie Kunz, the cascading strings of

51

Mantovani, and Ted Heath's big band. These records appeared in America on a new Decca subsidiary, London.

In America, CBS laboratories had been working on a 33 rpm long-playing record for years, and had cut all of their recordings onto 16" lacquers since 1939, believing that one day they could crack the case. Between the lab chief Peter Goldmark and his assistant Bill Bachman, the first Columbia "LPs" (Goldmark came up with the abbreviation) were released in 1948, with the first hit being the cast recording of South Pacific. They 'generously' offered RCA/Victor the opportunity to license the new technology. Not a chance. In 1949 RCA's secret project—codenamed Madame X—was launched on the world. Using the same microgroove technology, it was 7" across and played at 45 rpm.

The oldest 7" in my collection is Rosemary Clooney's Come On A-My House on the red Columbia label. It's from 1951, the year Columbia first pressed 45 rpm singles. 78s had hung on for a while (until the mid-1960s in India) with the last pressed in Britain in 1960. 78 collectors are a select breed, but some will pay plenty for Adam Faith's Poor Me or Billy Fury's My Christmas Prayer, released when pretty much everyone in Britain had switched to the two-speed record player we know and love.

The appeal of the 78 is undeniable—that cold, strange weight! the fragility!— and the low prices they go for on eBay doesn't put me off either. But everyone needs their cut-off points, and collecting 78s is probably a bridge too far for my sanity, my wallet, and the structural safety of my home. Will I end up scouring eBay for mint minus wax cylinders? No. I'll content myself for now with the lightweight 7" vinyl format, the red Parlophone of Adam Faith, the black-and-silver London of Del Shannon, pretty much anything on the Red Bird label. 40 years on, their mystery is intact, and the act of guiding the needle onto any of them is as close to religious practice as I'm ever going to get.

Painting hanging in Jazz Record Mart, Chicago, Illinois

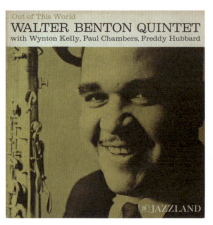

Black Power, Soundtrack, Orfeu, 1976

Walter Benton Quintet, *Out Of This World*, Jazzland, 1960

Billy Strayhorn Septet, *Cue For Saxophone*, London, 1959

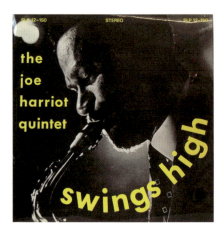

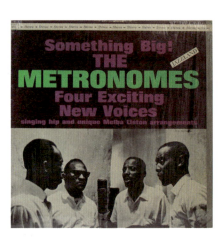

Joe Harriott Quintet, *Swings High*, Melodisc. 1967

The Mariachi Brass Featuring Chet Baker, *A Taste Of Tequila/Hats Off*, Ace

The Metronomes, *Something Big!*, Jazzland, 1962

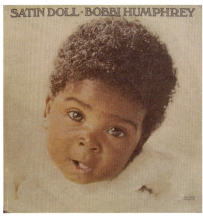

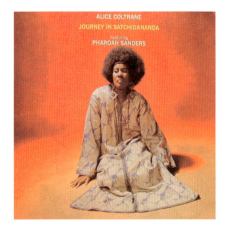

Oscar Brown, *Jr's Kicks*, BGP, 2004

Bobbi Humphey, *Satin Doll*, Blue Note, 1964

Alice Coltrane featuring Pharoah Sanders, *Journey in Satchidananda*, Impulse! Records, 1970

Stan Tracey Quartet, *Jazz Suite: Under Milk Wood*, Columbia, 1965

The Latin Jazz Quintet, *Latin Soul*

Graham Collier Septet, *Deep Dark Blue Centre*, Disconforme, 1967

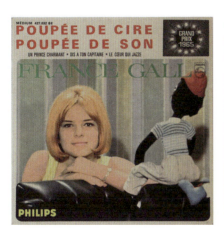

France Gall, *Poupee de Cire, Poupee de Son*, Philips, 1965

Nancy Sinatra, *Movin' With Nancy*, Reprise, 1967

'The Pink EP' by Teenage Jesus and the Jerks

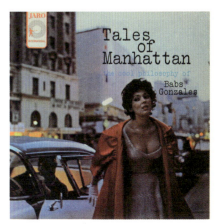

Amanaz, *Africa*, ZMPL/Shadoks, 1975

Roy Brooks, *Beat*, Workshop Jazz, 1963

Babs Gonzales, *Tales of Manhattan*, Jaro, 1959

::

A Conversation with Steve Krakow

::

What was the first record you ever bought?

Bought myself? At a flea market I got Journey's *Infinity*, Three Dog Night's *Golden Biscuits*, and Stories soundtrack—I just asked if they were rock LPs 'cause I wanted to get into 'rock'. I still get misty-eyed over the fuzz guitar on "Wheel in the Sky".

What are you collecting at the moment?

At the moment? Oh anything that's good I always say, and mainly 45s—but currently especially into what I call 'orchestral folk rock' a la Bob Lind, Bill Fay, some Jackie Deshannon—and anything emulating Phil Spector, plus Swedish communal psych jams, Scottish folk, country-psychedelic rock (pedal steel and fuzz) outsider/loner punk, obscure glam rock, avante composers (utilising drones usually), boogie rock from top 'til bottom, gutteral British freefest rock, any ace fingerpickers, froofy British psych, Brazilian pop, private pressed in-the-institution jams, devotional cosmic and/or free jazz.... I guess I started on oldies radio (Link Wray, Dave Clark 5, Beach Boys, etc) and classic rock (Iron Butterfly, Hendrix, Floyd) as a lad and just kept digging further—discovering the Velvets, Syd Barrett, and Nuggets as teenager were big for me.

Which is your favourite record store?

Oh, I worked at Reckless Records of London in Chicago for many years and had so many good finds and good times it would have to win out. But, I also love Record Dugout in Chicago, Crossroads and Mississippi in Portland, Lovegarden in Kansas, Amoeba and Saturn in Berkeley, Jive Time in Seattle, Rockit Scientist in New York, the junk shops of Knoxville, Grimey's in Nashville, Record Town in Arizona (in a strip mall) that closed down... sigh... having a good bathroom you can use while on tour also wins points.

Steve Krakow

What is your most treasured find?

Oh, that's tough—got amazing records at Reckless like beautiful copies of Neighb'rhood Children, Pink Fairies' *Never Neverland*, Lollipop Shoppe, The Forest, Idle Race, Amon Duul, Incredible Bongo Band, L'Histoire de Melodie Nelson, Jerry Moore, Mono Forever Changes and Easter Everywhere, Bruce Mackay, original Sun Ra *Saturns*.... But then finding kick-ass records in thrifts for so cheap has its own merits. I've found amazing 45s like Leviathan "Second Production" or the original *Kiddie a Go-Go* theme by Pandora and the Males (very Chicago-centric kid's TV show from the 1960s).

Name the most memorable episode set during record hunting days (a store, a personality, a conversation, a find, a fight, a dodgy deal, etc).

Ah, actually this 'super-fan' (a near-obsessive) of my band has a nameless/sign-less shop right next to a venue we were playing at in Oklahoma City—he had incredible records like Comus, Lincoln St Exit, Debris, Giles Giles and Fripp, Hugh Hopper, rare free jazz stuff. He traded us band merch for records, giving us incredible deals generally. He also tended bar at the venue, and was having girls flash us their breasts in exchange for shots (ok gross) and offered us every drug under the sun, and joked about us having his wife... a bit seedy, but again, good records were had (and no drugs OF COURSE). There was also this dude in Georgia who brought us to his living space in the back of the store (can't remember the name) which was his private record room and bedroom—it wasn't anything seedy—the whole room was lined top to ceiling with rare records, everything he pulled out was a heavy hitter... but there wasn't anything else in the room except a bed and records. This room's competition was only Thurston Moore and Byron Coley's Yodspace in North Hampton...whew...you need a ladder.

Has your approach towards collecting changed with the Internet?

Nope.

How have eBay and the Internet impacted on record collecting and the local store?

Oh plenty, a lot of the good records go on eBay immediately, but then again so many people are dumping old records and switching to their iPods basically, that folks can actually still find good vinyl, though some record stores are closing because a lot of folks do only want CDs or MP3s. But vinyl is eternal and will never decompose like digital files do.

What is the future for the record store and vinyl?

Well someone dubbed this the 'collectorage'—and that mentality has made things more expensive and lead to folks generally being aware that vinyl may have some value—but there will always be 'DJ's' in particular, the iconography has slipped pretty fully into the mainstream of 'scratchers' and the like—and serious audiophiles will always want things on vinyl, more and more kick-ass and rare records are being reissued on vinyl, so I think the future is looking pretty good.

Steve Krakow (aka Plastic Crimewave) has been carrying the Midwestern psychedelia torch for a number of years. He regularly performs with his band Plastic Crimewave Sound but is best known as the editor and publisher of Galactic Zoo Dossier.

::

A Conversation with Nick Luscombe

::

What was the first record you ever bought?

Giorgio Moroder's "From Here To Eternity" 7".

What are you collecting at the moment?

Like a lot of people at the start of 2008, I'm particularly inspired by the dubstep sound, so collecting various 12" singles when I see them. On my last trip to Japan, I found a great little book called *Electronic Music In The (Lost) World*. It is a total inspiration and has lead me to discover lots of great music from the late 1970s and 80s Japanese electronic/new wave scene. I've been scouring second hand record stores for records by P Model and Plastics plus video game music compilations. I have never been a 'label collector'—I don't have every record ever released on Warp for example... and I tend to buy records I like, as opposed to music I'm lead to believe I should own!

Which is your favourite record store?

In London—Sounds of the Universe; in Tokyo—Recofan.

Sounds of the Universe, London

Nick Luscombe

What is your most treasured find?

Most recently, a Japanese 12" picture disc called "Fly To The Future" issued by NEC for the 1985 Tsukubu Expo technology fair. It comes in a gatefold sleeve that folds out to show the inside of a spaceship. Does it ever get better than that?!

How have eBay and the Internet impacted on record collecting and the local store?

I do have the occasional eBay vinyl binge, often finding and ordering records I think I've lost—only to find them a few weeks later. Even with the Internet I still cant find a vinyl copy of *Romantic Attitude* by John Fitch and Associates. Also, I tend to do a fair amount of research online, which eventually leads me to the record store.

What is the future for the record store and vinyl?

There are too many 'diggers' out there for the vinyl format to vanish totally. I'm hopeful that specialist stores will survive. The mainstream record store could, and hopefully will, evolve to become a place where people still gather to discover and buy music, albeit on a different format. People like browsing, shopping and socialising, and the record store of the future could accommodate live performances, video and music downloads and consumer technology, all under one roof.

Nick Luscombe is a DJ in Britain, whose late night Flo Motion show on XFM was an influential source of leftfield club sounds for over six years. He currently hosts Flo Motion Live at Big Chill house, runs a folk-influenced club called Roots and Shoots, and releases Japanese artists through his vinyl-only label, Bambola Recordings.

A Conversation with Everett True

What was the first record you ever bought?

"The Biggest Blow" by The Sex Pistols (and Ronnie Biggs). I was an idiot. I was 17 and I knew it would be a question I would be asked in years to come. So I chose a Sex Pistols record. Damn it. The first record I heard, that made me understand, and fall deliriously in love with pop, was "Denis" by Blondie. Damn it. Even then I was too cool for my own good.

What are you collecting at the moment?

I don't collect per se, as I'm sent way too much stuff. But I particularly encourage folk like Dust-to-Digital, Numero Group and Germany's Trikont label to send me their magic collections of early to mid-twentieth century exotica, field recordings and unadorned pain: the sound quality is so refreshing. I have fairly extensive Nina Simone, Fall, Sonic Youth, Tom Waits, Shangri-La's, Buzzcocks, Legend!, Nick Cave, Half-Japanese and northern soul / Stax collections.

Which is your favourite record store?

There's only one (in London)—Rough Trade in Talbot Road. It's where my dreams gestated, and where I busked outside (as part of The Legend! And His Swinging Soul Sisters): it was a ritual, a reason to survive, that two-hour trip across London through the 1980s. Outside of London, there are tons.

Everett True

What is your most treasured find?

Um. Nothing beat the thrill of finding an original Ronettes album.

Name the most memorable episode set during record hunting days (a store, a personality, a conversation, a find, a fight, a dodgy deal, etc).

Ha. A fight, huh? Outside Rough Trade Records— "five mods picked on one punk, I wondered if I should get involved and try and stop it, but violence would have created more violence…" Or something. It was that memorable an incident that Creation Records was formed to release the song inspired by it. Ha! Aside from that, buying all my cassette tapes in cassette tape heyday from Jim (Foetus) Thirwell's counter in Virgin Oxford Walk and being forced by same to allow Throbbing Gristle to sign my copy of *Heathen Earth* because cameras were rolling and I was the only fan to show up. Or perhaps watching Huggy Bear from behind the counter in Rough Trade, Covent Garden. Or leaving my cherished (and expensive) Snakefinger coloured-vinyl single "The Spot" on top of my mate Geoff's car as we drove off from Talbot Road.

Has your approach towards collecting changed with the Internet? How have eBay and the Internet impacted on record collecting and the local store?

EBay is fun for a short while, but then you realise it reduces the thrill, being able to access everything you ever wanted when you were so much younger. If I still bought records, doubtless I would crave human contact and taste-making.

What is the future for the record store and vinyl?

Vinyl is way superior to CD: it is the CD manufacturers who should be concerned, as more and more people realise increasingly what a rubbish format it's always been. Record stores are hardly going to disappear now, are they?

Everett True, aka Jerry Thackray, is a British music journalist, whose controversial voice made an impact across a range of music papers, including the *NME* and *Melody Maker*, throughout the 1980s. He currently edits *Plan B* magazine, and is the author of several books (his latest release being 2006's *Nirvana: The True Story*).

David Lashmar in Beano's, Croydon, London

DAVID LASHMAR

The trouble is... we have bred a new power generation that has lost its desire for artistic possessions.

It seems most of the air breathers who can walk fairly upright and that were born in the last 30 years, have wires in their ears. The whole of their life is on their iPod and their phone. Photos, friends and music.

For them there is no need to ever own a record or a CD when they can download something the record companies convince them is 'essential', and that can be consumed with little effort. Sort of an audio Big Mac.

To them, 'browsing' is something to do with computers rather than a pastime.

They will never know the joy of flicking through a rack of records, being captivated by cover artwork and reading the sleeve notes. Of getting the record home, sliding it reverentially out of its cover and then out of its inner sleeve, marveling at the lustre of the grooves. The sacrificial offering onto the altar of the turntable, the gentle penetration of the spindle, the lowering of the arm and the total bliss of being part of an actual performance that you have helped to complete. This baptismal immersion into sonic joy will never leave you. The day you bought the record, where you were, what you were wearing and who was in your heart, will be etched into your soul, as well defined as the grooves that are pressed into your record.

I urge you to think before you surrender totally to the digital god who merely occupies a slice of your hard-drive. There is more, much more, out there than will ever reach your ears via a pair of white wires, but you will have to use your hands and your desire to be different.

David Lashmar is owner and founder of Beano's in Croydon, one of Britain's best-loved second-hand record shops.

STUART BAKER

I run a record shop called Sounds of The Universe and a label called Soul Jazz Records. I started the shop when my friend, Alec Liddell, and myself first travelled to America to buy second-hand records to sell in Britain. I think it was 1990. This was before the Internet, mobile phones, cheap airlines and CDs were just becoming the mainstream.

We had found a book called Record Shops in the USA and we used this as a guide. We bought our plane tickets from Polo Express, a company that gave you cheap tickets in exchange for carrying British Airways documents. It was quite funny because you had to wear a suit and take out your earrings (for some reason I had seven). Sometimes there would be nothing to take so you could go into the loos at the airport and change back into jeans. So I think the ticket was £100. We flew to New York (we didn't hang around here) and hired a car. Someone in a record shop in Britain had casually said, "if you go to a place like St Louis, all the records are $1". So off we went! Needless to say they weren't $1 at all.

I would say it's the most fun I've ever had, driving to a town in America, going to a telephone kiosk and looking up record shops to visit in the town, going from one shop to another as fast as you can so as to reach another town the same day. Sometimes you'd look in the yellow pages at your hotel and the page with record shops would be torn out and you'd know you weren't the first!

A funny time we were in a shop in Chicago—the late Ruby Sales, whose slogan "We're going out for Business", was made to look on a sale sign like "We're going out of business" suggested we see his son. "He's got a load of crap but you may find something". That was enough for us and off we went. The building was on the edge of the city, a huge factory and we had to climb into a 30 feet wide goods lift to get to the top floor. Everything was on pallets and as we looked through the records we heard a rumble. A few seconds later a huge iron ball came through one of the walls! "Don't worry, they are starting to knock the building down", said the son. Some good records though.

Stuart Baker is the owner of Sounds of the Universe, and runs Soul Jazz Records in Britain.

Sahib Shihab, *Sentiments*, Atlantic, 1971

I*mpala Syndrome*, Soundtrack, Parallax, 1969

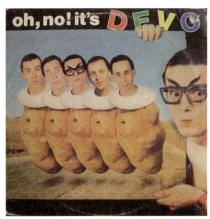

Devo, *Oh No! It's Devo*, Virgin

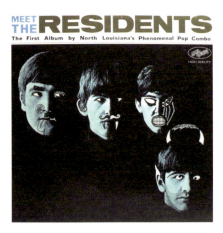

The Residents, *Meet The Residents*, Ralph Records, 1974

V/A, *PopShopping*, Crippled Dick Hot Wax, 2000

Lee Morgan, *Expoobident*, Vee-Jay, 1960

Dick Dale, *Surfer's Guitar*, Surf Records

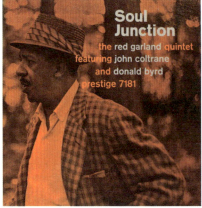

Red Garland Quintet, *Soul Junction*, Prestige. 1957

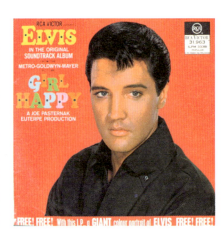

Elvis Presley, *Happy Girl*, RCA Victor, 1965

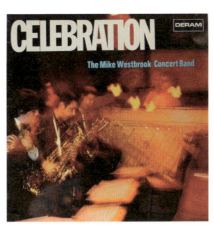

Paul Gonsalves Quartet, *Boom-Jackie Boom-Chick*,
Vocalion, 1963.

The Mike Westbrook Concert Band, *Celebration*,
Deram, 1967

Gordon Beck Quartet, *Experiment with Pops*, Major
Minor, 1968

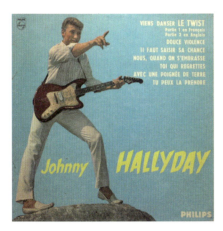

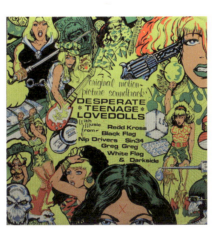

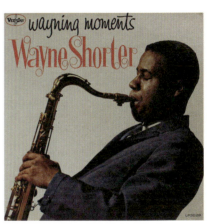

Johnny Hallyday, *Viens Danser LeTwist*, Philips, 1964

Desperate Teenage Lovedolls, Soundtrack, SST, 1986

Wayne Shorter, *Wayning Moments*, Vee-Jay, 1962

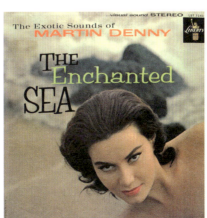

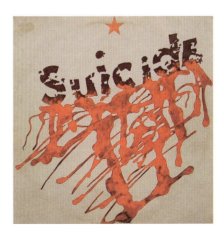

The Cramps, *Creature from the Black Leather Lagoon*,
Enigma, 1990

Martin Denny, *The Enchanted Sea*, Liberty, 1960

Suicide, Soundtrack, Red Star, 1977

MY LIFE IN RECORD STORES: A CAUTIONARY TALE

By Byron Coley

Over the last few years there has been a wild burst of hand wringing over the presumptive fate of independent record stores. Most people seem to agree that they're dead or dying (in both conceptual and quotidian terms), and I suppose that's true. But only in the sense that all of us are either dead or dying. *We're all in various stages of decay—you, me, that sad guy from* High Fidelity—*all of us*. Big deal. It's just the natural order of things. It's true that there currently seem to be fewer people who are interested in records per se, but that is largely a result of the music industry's idiotic drive to shoot itself in every foot. Don't blame me, or my record scum buddies. We're still as idiotically interested in fetishising vinyl product as we ever were, but we're all getting goddamned old, and we're not being replaced in a fast and timely manner. The music industry screwed total pooch when they decided to digitise product in order to increase short-term profit margins.

Ask anyone who really knows anything about music and they'll tell you the same thing—CDs suck. I mean, they're okay as stand-ins for cassettes or 8 track tapes or those old hip pocket singles, but they are supremely null as objects. There have been some interesting packages for a few of them—Alan Silva's paint-spattered *Treasure Box*, the Boredoms' mechanically squeaking *Vision Creation Newsun*, and Climax Golden Twins' sleep-ready *Lovely* come readily to mind, but most CDs are largely inert—designed merely to carry sounds in the cheapest, most dry-assed way imaginable.

They have no magic, no soul and no interest except as sonic delivery vehicles. If you are just a music lover, this might conceivably be fulfilling, but if you are a record lover, a wallower in the physicality of musical artefacts, then they're just bland. They are also the root cause of the decline of independent record stores (so called, although, this is not as clear a fact as it might seem, but I digress).

It would be tough for me to figure out how much time I've spent lollygagging in the bowels of independent record stores over the past four and a half decades, but it is a time span that would have to be measured in years. There have been periods of my life where my entire existence revolved around the damn things. They represented the main places where I hung out—learning all sorts of useless information, working out my own crude aesthetic vocabulary, and meeting some of my most enduring friends (and enemies). I have whiled away vast tracts of my existence in places like San Francisco's Aquarius, Los Angeles' Rhino, Boston's In Your Ear, and millions of points in between. And truthfully, I don't regret many of these moments. Indeed, I can remember a shocking number of such places and times with a clarity that surprises me. One can only assume I tended to shop and work while sober. Not always, but mostly.

The first record store I remember was called Post's Electronics in Butler, New Jersey. Post's Electronics was primarily an

appliance store. They sold hi-fi equipment, refrigerators, electric organs, and had a separate section devoted to long-playing records, in both monophonic and stereophonic configurations (this was back when stereo LPs had a list price of a dollar more than mono ones). When my parents would go to Butler to shop, I would tag along and head into Post's to examine their stock. Most of it was dull adult pop—Perry Como, Doris Day, Mitch Miller and the like—but they also carried some of the rock records that were starting to chart around that time. The Beatles had just made their life-changing appearances on *The Ed Sullivan Show* but, to be honest, I loathed them. It was early 1964, and my interests lay not in the grey fog of Britain, but in the sunny, sandy warmth of southern California. Surf and hot-rod music—whether the vocal ambrosia of Jan & Dean and the Beach Boys, or the hard-edged instrumentals of the Ventures—held me in sway. When the first Rip Chords LP appeared, its cover a testament to the raw power of the 1963 Shelby Cobra, I was totally hooked. I knew somehow this had to be the first album I owned, and by late Spring of 1964, it was.

I can't remember—and can scarcely imagine—what I must have done to save the money to buy that record. I was seven at the time, and my allowance was ¢35 a week. *Mad* magazine came out once a month at ¢25 an issue. A Heath Bar cost five. A stereo copy of *Hey Little Cobra and Other Hot Rod Hits* was $4.98. You do the math. I know there must have been some serious privation involved in buying this record, but all I remember is going into Post's and staring at the cover week after week, dreaming of the day it would be mine.

I was so excited by my purchase, and the stereo copy sounded so incredibly good on my dad's Magnavox console hi-fi, that I immediately started planning my next purchase. Some of my friends were into singles, which could be purchased at a local soda fountain/candy shop called the Kin-Lon Spa. But there was little sense of discovery or exploration associated with singles. A single had two songs. Of those, one was well-known, leaving little chance for serendipitous discovery. Similarly, few singles even had picture sleeves, and those that did were usually pretty light on text. When you held an album in your hands, even if you knew 'the hit', that meant there'd probably be 11 songs about which you knew naught. The Rip Chords sang, not only their hit, but such wonderful never-to-be-singles tunes as "Trophy Machine" and "Queen". There was also the pleasure of reading whatever notes were on the back of the album jacket—whether simply song credits or short essays about the musicians and the scenes from which

they came. Combined with the gorgeous, shiny square-foot cover image, designed to ensnare eyes and imaginations alike, I was a willing captive of the LP format. Call it the Stockholm Syndrome if you insist, I don't give a tinker's cuss.

In the early days of the 'British Invasion', the Kin-Lon Spa began to carry LPs as well as singles, but their sales presentation was totally half-assed. They housed the records in spinning metal racks, more suitable for comic books or paperbacks, so I didn't switch allegiance from Post's. Until, that is, I discovered the Colonial Toy Shop in Pompton Lake. Like Post's, the Colonial was a multi-purpose store. You could buy Weirdos model kits there and board games and stuff, but they also had a very nice selection of rock 'n' roll singles and albums that grew over the years, until it eventually took over the whole store. Initially, the record aisles were a little dark, and the clerks seemed to know more about Lionel trains than they did about the Yardbirds, but the place was very cool. It was also in the same block as the area's only movie theatre at the time, so it was a perfect place to hang out while waiting for our moms to pick us up after the latest Bond flick.

But the main source for records in those days was more likely to be department stores. Places like Korvette's and Two Guys had what seemed like huge, well-lit, well-organised record sections, and they featured relatively deep stock, meaning they might have all of the first three albums by The Animals. This doesn't seem so radical now, but at the time, it was revelatory. As was our subsequent discovery of the Sam Goody store in Paramus. Sam Goody was a small independent east coast chain at the time, numbering less than 20 stores, which prided itself on carrying everything. It didn't seem possible that more records existed than Goody's stocked. The selection was really first rate. But they didn't discount records the way the department stores did. Most of Goody's offerings were sold for list price or close to it. At department stores, new titles were offered at significant discounts (a foreshadowing of big box things to come, although we didn't know it at the time). Still, the Sam Goody flagship store on 49th Street in Manhattan was an awe-inspiring place. Whether you bought anything or not, it was inspirational to just be in the company of all that music. Its proximity provided a tangible charge.

The thrill of proximity remained true when I went away to school in the fall of 1969. I got a gig at the school radio station, and volunteered to clerk at the record store they ran as a fundraising tool. The store was staffed entirely by station DJs and, although our stock was pretty limited,

Play only 78s
on this turn-
table

↓

it was carefully chosen and thoroughly vetted by committee. It was the first small record store I'd ever been in where it was considered cool to ask questions (and even cooler to be able to answer them). Some student might come in and be snared by the Renee Magritte cover art on the *Bec-Ola* album by the Jeff Beck Group. What a pleasure it was to be able to inform the guy (the school was still all-male) that Beck had been one of the guitarists in the Yardbirds. And that he, like Clapton before him and Page soon after, had decided to try something a little less pop-oriented. 'Progressive blues' we called it. "With a killer young singer."

I had started to pick up the verbiage of rock-speak a couple of years earlier, during my junior high school days. There was one serious rock magazine then, *Crawdaddy*, but it was something I was only able to access via one of my friend's older brothers, who was very serious about his music. Unfortunately, he didn't often countenance us going through his stuff. Still, there was a weekly free music paper called *Go* that was sponsored by various radio stations across the country (in my case, WMCA-AM, home of The Good Guys). It was available at Village Music in Montclair, handily located right across the parking lot from where I had my piano lessons every Wednesday. Thus, I was able to get my hands on it regularly, and I poured through its stories and reviews, reading and re-reading articles about bands I'd neither heard nor heard of, trying to put it all together. I would even type up my own occasional musical reports on my portable Smith-Corona. Thankfully, no copies of these missives remain extant.

Village Music had probably been the first independent record store (that was nothing but a record store) I ever patronised on a regular basis. But the owner was kind of grumpy, and their stock focused heavily on classical LPs and rock singles, so it never fully engaged me as anything other than a source for *Go* magazine. But the radio station's store, located in the basement of a dorm whose name escapes me, was a wonderful swamp in which to submerge.

It's weird thinking back, but, because the store was basically a fundraising wing of the station, in-store play was limited to records that the staff would haul down from the station's library or from our own collections. Shifts were fairly short, with three of us working at a time, managing the fortunes of a couple of hundred albums, but whoever was on duty would get to play one side of a record. I recall there was a lot of running back and forth between the store and the station,

getting open copies of records and whatnot. I wasn't there for long, but it was a hell of a fertile scene, and it was where I first hatched the notion that a record store should function as a de facto clubhouse for folks who lacked the social skills to interact with flesh and blood as nimbly as they could with vinyl.

Back in Butler in the early 1970s, a record store called Mr Muck's opened. It was run out of a house by a couple of young hippies (or virtual hippies) and combined certain aspects of a head shop with a record store. This struck me as an excellent hybrid, but one unfortunate aspect of the shop was the Catholic tastes of the proprietors. This was an era when singer-songwriterism was viewed as the pinnacle of contemporary culture. But if you were reading *Creem* magazine, a newly nationalised, Detroit-based music rag filled with rants and cussing and attitude, it was pretty tough to accept the notion that James Taylor was the answer to anyone's question. You'd read about bands like the Flamin' Groovies or the Stooges, but nobody carried their records. Oh, it's true Sam Goody did, and they had opened a branch store in a mall in Wayne, but I was never very comfortable breathing the dead air that seemed to fill every mall I ever entered. It might be necessary to venture into one for emergencies (like when you needed to get a Captain Beefheart cassette on short notice), but they were no place to hang out. This kind of put the squeeze on me for a while. I couldn't handle the music they were playing in the hippie shops, but I couldn't bear the flourescent lights of the alternatives.

I stopped shopping locally for a while and took my business into Manhattan every weekend. Amazing used record stores started cropping up. Places like Freebeing on Second Avenue, where you could find review copies of excellent and/or bizarre records for a couple of bucks. And it was always a treat to go into Village Oldies, where Lenny Kaye worked, to seek out copies of the strange novelty singles that Howard Smith played on his Sunday night radio show on WABC-FM, and to eavesdrop on the wild, arcane garage band singles that Lenny would play and talk about with his cronies. When I went to college in western Massachusetts, there turned out to be several good record stores in the area, but the best was definitely Sun Music in Amherst. It was the pre-dawn of the punk era, and Sun's proprietor, Mike Kostek, was a guy who was interested and knowledgeable about strange records of all kinds. Sun was the kind of place where you could hang out and argue for hours about the relative merits of Velvet Underground songs (the original velvet Underground Appreciation Society was actually born out of that store),

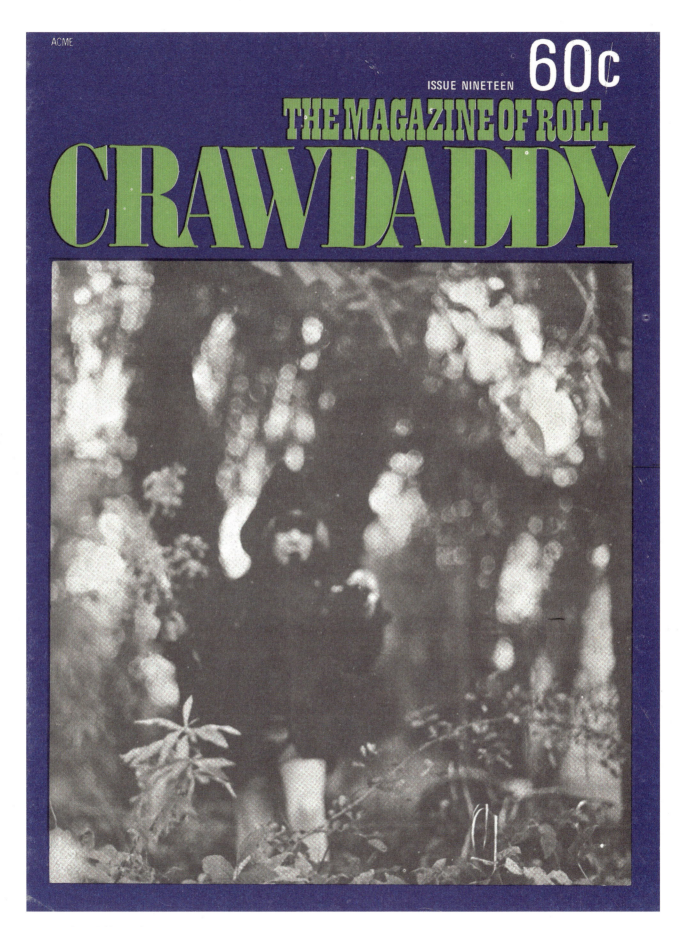

ACME

ISSUE NINETEEN

60c

THE MAGAZINE OF ROLL
CRAWDADDY

Front cover of *Crawdaddy* Magazine, Issue 19, 1968

and I can still remember the day when Kostek came back from a flea market with the first known copy of the Shaggs' *Philosophy of the World* LP. The Shaggs were a parent-financed group of sisters from New Hampshire, whose musical primitivism was so complete that it was possible to believe it to be imbued with genius. When that album was played at Sun, people would consistently stop in their tracks, cock their heads and ask, "What the fuck is that?". This was a question that could not be answered in short form, but no one who shopped at Sun minded. We all fancied ourselves to be experts on one or another small corner of the universe, and when someone pushed the right button, they had better be prepared for discourse.

Sun was one of the great stores of its era, and the first shop besides Berkeley's Rather Ripped to actually stock records by the Residents. Half Japanese, Metal Urbain, Big Star, Sun Ra—these were all figures prominent in the hagiography of Sun's aesthetic. There was a lot of weird information and energy to soak up in that shop.

I missed the place acutely when I moved out to San Francisco and ended up having to work in lame chain stores to support myself. But, I'd sometimes take my cheques directly to the old Aquarius on Castro Street, and turn them into vinyl on the spot. By the latter part of the 1970s, the world punk explosion was in full swing and there were more amazing singles coming out than anyone could possibly fathom. San Francisco and Berkeley were both excellent record towns anyway, filled with specialty used stores and odd neighbourhood places where you could turn up incredible gems. After a while, I no longer bothered to work, and spent my time trading and selling records between different stores in the Bay Area. Some places liked jazz and hated folk. Other places loved folk and hated rock. Almost all the older guys hated punk. If you knew what you were doing, it was possible to comb ¢99 bins in certain stores and discover things that were gold at shops on the other side of the bay. I won't say there was decent money in it, but my rent was only $80 a month, one of the bartenders at the Mabuhay accepted foodstamps as tender, and you could sell plasma twice a week down on Mission. Who needed money?

The best stores in the Bay Area were probably Rather Ripped in Berkeley and Aquarius in San Francisco. Both these stores combined well-chosen used records with wild, obscure new stuff that ranged from punk to bizarre experimental noise to avant garde jazz to homemade records that were as hard to describe as they were to sell. And the clerks were insanely

knowledgeable about their fields of expertise. They were intimidating and funny and full of crackpot theories, and it was really a pleasure to hang back, chuckle appreciatively and just soak up the vibe.

When I moved back to New York, that vibe was what I missed most. There are always great stores in New York, but the guys who run them forever seem to be working one angle or another. I mean, to me, a place like Bleecker Bob's—legendary though it might be—was a store I would only visit as a last resort, if no one else in town was able to conjure up the record. The people who worked in these stores really bummed me out. Even later, when I'd hang around at Venus or Midnight, I always felt as though someone was trying to hustle me. And usually they were. But the 1980s were really the dawn of serious record collecting, and man, if you kept your eyes peeled, remained diligent and knew what it was you were looking at—it was possible to get anything (ANYTHING) in New York.

Obviously, when I say that the 1980s were the dawn of serious collecting, there will be a lot of people who take issue with that. Okay. I admit it, there was lots of collecting going on before that. But it didn't really start to get interesting (to me, anyway) until the 1980s. I first became aware of collector's fanzines and rare record dealers in the early 1970s. But at that time, the stuff that people were collecting was doo wop, rockabilly, pre-war blues, jazz 78s, original cast recordings, classical, and maybe the occasional psychedelic or garage single. The bulk of this shit was way outside my own interests.

It started to change as the 1970s went along. Especially after Lenny Kaye curated the Nuggets comp for Elektra, then helped put out that first Patti Smith Group single on Mer, the pace began to pick up. There started to be lots of fanzines dedicated both to 1960s garage rock (still one of my fave genres) and the burgeoning contemporary underground (which meant only that the bands were not popular). By the time the early 1980s arrived, people had started to discover just how much stuff of this ilk there was, and were seriously becoming interested in figuring out how it flowed from place to place, how it evolved, and what it was about. Fanzines were one of the main foci of these efforts, but they were matched by the work of the best independent record stores. This was a change that was becoming obvious in New York, but it was even more evident when I moved to Boston in 1980. Boston and Cambridge had always been decent towns for

Previous Pages: Stacks in Jazz Record Mart, Chicago, Illinois
Opposite: Signage in Rather Ripped, Berkeley, California

I'D RATHER BE RIPPED
RECORDS
NORTHSIDE • BERKELEY
"THE BEST LITTLE RECORD STORE YOU EVER SAW"

used records, but for a long time the best place for new stuff was the Harvard Co-op. This started to change with the opening of two distinctly different stores on Newbury Street. The first was Newbury Comics, a kind of poncey place where you could watch bored band members lolling around, pretending they knew a lot about music. There were a few okay clerks there—mostly DJs—but the good records usually got short-stopped before they hit the racks, and the stuff in the bins was generally lackluster. They also sold comic books and various other kinds of crap, which seemed lame to me at the time, but this approach seems to have served them well, since they turned into a small chain here in New England and are still going strong. But a much better store was just down the street, and called Rebop. It was run by two hardcore music addicts, who really knew their shit, and the couple of clerks they had were equally up-to-snuff. One of them, Dan Ireton, recording under the name Dredd Foole (as he still does today) went on to become one of the godfathers of the whole new weird America movement. But I'm getting ahead of myself. In 1980, Rebop was just a cool store, mixing new and used stock with a crazy assortment of punk singles, psychedelic re-issues, and obscure fanzines. I could stand there all day, smoking Camels with owner, Bill Poczik, listening to him wax enthusiastic about everything from the British folk band, the Trees, to the White Panther churn of Detroit's The Up. As is true of all the best stores, I learned a lot hanging around Rebop. I was sad as hell when they closed up, but Newbury Street rents had started to rise even down at the cheap end of the street. The yuppies were on the march, turning crappy neighborhoods into their personal mock-bohemian fiefdoms, and nothing was going to stop them. By the time they turned their sites on Rebop's block, I had already moved to Los Angeles, so I was unable to avail myself of the store's closing sale. Bummer.

At that time (1981), Los Angeles had both sprawling new and used stores that would have been beyond imagining in the claustrophobic, high-priced real estate setting of Manhattan or downtown Boston, as well as an amazing array of specialty stores, some of which sold singles so local that no other stores could get them. One of the first things I did after moving there was to interview the band Black Flag. In the course of our talk, I asked bassist Chuck Dukowksi if he could recommend a record store. He said, "Oh, Zed's in Long Beach is great". "Yeah, but isn't that kinda far?" I asked. "No way", he said. "Just take the 405 south to the Long Beach Freeway. It's right off of there." In traffic, this drive took me about an hour. The next time I saw Dukowksi, I

asked if he'd been pulling my joint. "That drive to Zed's took me an hour", I said. "See, I told you it wasn't far", he answered.

I discovered that in Southern California, it was no big deal to drive an hour for a gig or a record store or anything else. It was just part of the flow. And even though the area was vast, stores like Poo Bah in Pasadena, Vinyl Fetish in Hollywood, Rhino in Westwood and Zed's in Long Beach were all considered local. It was different, but it wasn't hard to get used to. I lived in Santa Monica, so Rhino became my local haunt. At first I was just a customer. In those days I was getting review copies of 50 to a hundred strange European imports every week. I'd keep the cream of them, but drop the rest off as trade-ins every weekend. The indie/import buyer at that time was guitarist, Nels Cline. After I'd been a regular for a few months, he knew who I was and we started talking. He knew my work situation wasn't superb just then, so when Steve Wynn was preparing to quit his position in order to focus full-time on the Dream Syndicate, he asked if I wanted the job. Although it didn't pay much, it was such a plum gig that available spots were passed only to regular customers who had proved their mettle. And it was a great set-up.

Everyone who worked at Rhino had a niche. Each person was expected to master one of the genres the store carried, and to be able to do any orders that might be needed, set up related promotions and window displays, and also to be able to buy used vinyl, regardless of category. There was an apprenticeship period, but after that I was more or less let loose to buy whatever American indie label stuff I wanted. I could drive out to the Bomp warehouse with a blank cheque, spend a couple of hours talking to Greg and Suzi Shaw, and come back with a trove of singles that hadn't been available anywhere for years. I could call up Glen Danzig from the Misfits or Corey Rusk from the Necros and order a box of whatever they had handy. Other people were doing similar things with jazz and blues and African music and reggae and folk, and it was a pretty amazing blend of stuff. The store had also developed the philosophy (similar to the one Nick Hornsby later explored in *High Fidelity*) that the customer is not always right, and to pretend otherwise is bullshit. Some people hung out there just to be abused by the clerks. I guess they appreciated the acknowledgement, no matter what form it took. But Rhino was a nexus of activity on the West Side. Most of the clerks there were either musicians, writers or DJs. The rest were guys who really knew a lot about music. Tons of musicians used to hang out there, to buy and sell records, or just listen to the

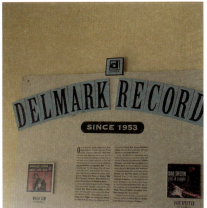

Top Left: Rockaway Records, Silverlake, California
Middle Left: Archive of Popular Music, New York
Bottom Left: Jazz Record Mart, Chicago, Illinois

Top Middle: Delmark Records, Chicago, Illinois
Centre: Jazz Record Mart, Chicago, Illinois
Bottom Middle: Reckless Records, Chicago, Illinois

Top Right: Rockaway Records, Silverlake, California
Middle Right: Yale Evelevand his record collection, Manhattan, New York
Bottom Right: Aquarius Records, San Francisco, California

bullshit. It's pretty wild to remember. It was a very cool spot. When I went back to Boston in 1984, there was really nothing comparable. Rebop was long gone, and Newbury Comics had evolved into something even more useless than it had been before. I was mostly busy with writing work for a while, but I spent time checking out the area's stores, using the method that had worked for me in Los Angeles, I'd just take a pile of oddball promo records somewhere and see if the clerk had any idea what they were. In the days before the Internet made everyone a pseudo-expert and pseudo-record dealer, it was a pretty good way to get a feel for the situation.

By this process, I determined that In Your Ear—a classic mix of weird new records and used ones—was Boston's best bet. The second of the store's several locations, occupying a large, sunny storefront near Boston University, was the one at which I worked. Other clerks tended to be either college DJs or musicians, with a few hardened record geeks thrown into the mix. I did specialty ordering there for a while, then started up a mail order rare record business with a friend. There had been a hardcore compilation a few years earlier called *This is Boston, Not LA*, that about summed up my feelings about actually working at a store. Rhino had been exciting. You never knew when Kareem Abdul-Jabbar might drop in to spend a few thousand dollars on crappy soul-jazz records. Or you'd get invited to go bowling with Richard Thompson. It was a damn interesting place to be. There was nowhere in Boston that could hope to offer similar entertainment value. I also realised, as I closed in on 30, that I knew way too much about records. I couldn't bear to have people who were only mildly interested in music ask me any questions about the stuff. Unless it was an extremely attractive woman, I was unable to choke back the bile of contempt that automatically rose in my throat.

I spent the next few years buying records like a madman, as idiots sold off all their best LPs to replace them with CDs. Some people talk about this as a golden era for record stores, but I'm not sure that's true. Yes, it was possible to make a lot of money at used stores, spinning shit into gold (and vice versa), but there was so much new stuff coming out that it threatened to swamp everything. By the time the 1990s rolled around. I was getting so many promos that the people who worked at my local post office became abusive if I went out of town for a day or two. So much was being released at such a frantic pace, and so much of it was pretty good, that it became progressively harder to have enough time to figure out which of the things might actually be great. I didn't really feel as though there were any stores that could provide real answers either.

In New York, there had been a trend towards smaller and smaller areas of specialisation. Venus had a great handle on a specific kind of British DIY crap. Midnight was an excellent place to find garage stuff of all eras. But if you wanted avant garde jazz, you had to go to SoHo Music Gallery, or try to weasel your way into NMDS. And if you wanted bizarre psychedelic or folk stuff, you had to comb the record boxes on St Marks Place. It was no longer possible for one single store to contain everything hip and good, as it had been (or seemingly so) back in the heyday of Rather Ripped and Aquarius. Things had just gotten too spread out. The introduction of the CD meant that labels were mining every inch of their back catalogue they could lay their hands on. Records so arcane that they had barely existed, were now available in bright digital versions of themselves for a mere fraction of their worth as artefacts.

This was interesting in a way, but it also removed a lot of the mystery that had been a part of the record store experience. The Internet started to bloom in the same period, and even more mystery was stripped from the process. Now, if you found a record, you could put it on hold at a store and go home to check and see what it was worth, what it was about and all that. The fact that the vast majority of information on the web is bullshit didn't have much effect on its ability to replicate itself like a virus. Once a single person describes Alistair Anderson (a guy who play concertina in the English traditional style) as "an amazing female acid folk vocalist", there's no way to take it back. That little piece of bullshit is going to pop up now and then as long as anyone is interested in Alistair. But no one seemed particularly abashed by the fact that the web was so choked with bad information. They swallowed it the same way they swallowed the inflated prices of CDs (at least for a while) and the same way they swallow the recommendations of Amazon.com (ghost record clerk to the world). Even this far into the history of Amazon's Boolean logic, the site's powers of recommendation fall far below that of one decent record store clerk.

The problem has become that decent record store clerks are so few and far between that people no longer expect to find them. This was amply demonstrated by my last experiments in hands-on retail salesmanship. Sometime in the 1990s, I started to get a lot of grief about the number of records I had in the house, the barn, the garage, and various storage spaces. When I'd return home with a cache of great new finds, I was greeted, not as a successful hunter-gatherer, but as an eccentric hoarder of mystery objects. In order to cover my actions,

208 EAST 6TH STREET
SIDE A
SINCE 1985
JUST RECORDS
SELLIN' & BUYIN'
BUYIN' & SELLIN'
Telephone
212 – 533 – 8007
OPEN
TUESDAY-SATURDAY
12pm – 7pm
SUNDAY
1pm – 7pm
IN VINYL WE TRUST
IN VINYL WE TRUST

I began to tell my family I was just putting together stock for "the store". What store? Well, the one I planning to open. I discussed this gambit with a friend of mine who was having similar reactions to his record buying habits. He agreed it was a good one. Some time passed quietly, then the questions began. When would this record store appear?

Eventually, we had to shit or get off the pot, as they say. We opened a small record store in an old grist mill that functioned primarily as a used book store, way out in the woods of New England. For the location, our stock was breathtaking, if I do say so myself. People would wander in and flip through the racks, unable to figure out what a single one of these records actually was. It was great. There is a certain type of record store customer who just comes in to make conversation. He (it's almost never a she) will come to the counter with some record or another, not with any real thought of buying it, but simply to make a bunch of noise discussing its relative merits. The vast majority of these guys are jerk-offs whose real knowledge would fit in a thimble. Our store—the Ecstatic Yod Mill Outlet—totally stumped them. These types could not find a single thing they'd ever heard or even read about. It was fantastic to watch them—slowly realising that they were as far out of their depth as the average jack-ass leaf-peeper, who'd stop in and ask "Hey, do you have any $3 Mozart CDs?". Eventually, the financial pain of having to meet a payroll outweighed these cheap thrills, and we decided to recreate the store in what we called "the Japanese style". This meant we moved to the fourth floor of an old industrial building, with no sign anywhere that we existed as a business. Anyone who can find us is obviously interested in finding us because they know what we have. It has been a workable solution. I mean, we don't get many customers, but the ones we do get are real quality, if you know what I mean.

But we're able to do this because it's really just a hobby for us. We get a kick out of it and do it pretty much so we'll have a guaranteed place to hang out. Now The Man really can't bust our music! It's a different story for anyone who hopes to make a living in the business, unless they're very nimble and smart. There are a lot of reasons for this, but most of them are financial. The average person doesn't really care much about music, except as it can be used as a soundtrack to their daily lives. They have no real interest in any kind of value-added artefact. They just want to hear the song they want to hear, when they want to hear it. Back when I was first getting into albums, these were the people who were happy buying singles. And they actually kept buying singles

(even in such idiot formats as cassettes and CDs) until the record industry, in their infinite greed, decided they weren't making enough money off of singles. If people wanted one song, they'd just have to buy the whole album at whatever ridiculous rip-off price the industry set for the ten cents of plastic they extruded to meet the market's demands. This choice will prove to be their downfall.

The music industry's decision to ignore the person who just wants a single song, without any of its context, made the bulk of the casual audience start thinking that downloading might not be such a bad idea after all. MP3s didn't sound much worse than their shitty stereos, so what the heck? Of course, you might argue that the industry had already destroyed (or at least cheapened) the music's context by their initial decision to move to the CD. The CD as a delivery form destroys the conceptual basis of the album as being comprised of two distinctly programmed suites of music with an implicit narrative arc. It just throws everything into a blender and adds bonus tracks, regardless of what that might do to the music's pacing. Context? What's that?

These customers (who didn't give a shit about context anyway) were driven from the stores corporate greed-heads, and this was a customer base that kept a lot of independent stores afloat, especially in secondary markets. Unless you were in a big city, where you could try to capture a small corner of a huge market, independent stores had to cater to everyone. In your heart, you might want to carry nothing but records somehow related to Nick Cave and all his fellow travellers, but in order to do this, you'd have to have a store that dedicated the other 90 per cent of its floor space to music that the average person knew about and wanted. It was a balance that was always pleasing to see when travelling. You'd walk into a mom and pop store in Topeka, Kansas, and stroll down rows of dull commercial country music, before finding an obscure corner crammed with whatever records happened to obsess the owner. It could be surf or klezmer or goth, but it was always cool, always told you that there was someone here who really loved music. And someone who had to be polite to everyone who walked in looking for the latest boy-pop record, because that's what pays the rent. These customers disappeared when it transpired that the only place they could get individual songs was from iTunes.

The next group of lost customers is the one sucked away by Amazon, Best Buy, eBay and Wal-Mart. These were the industry's bread and butter, although I'm not sure they were

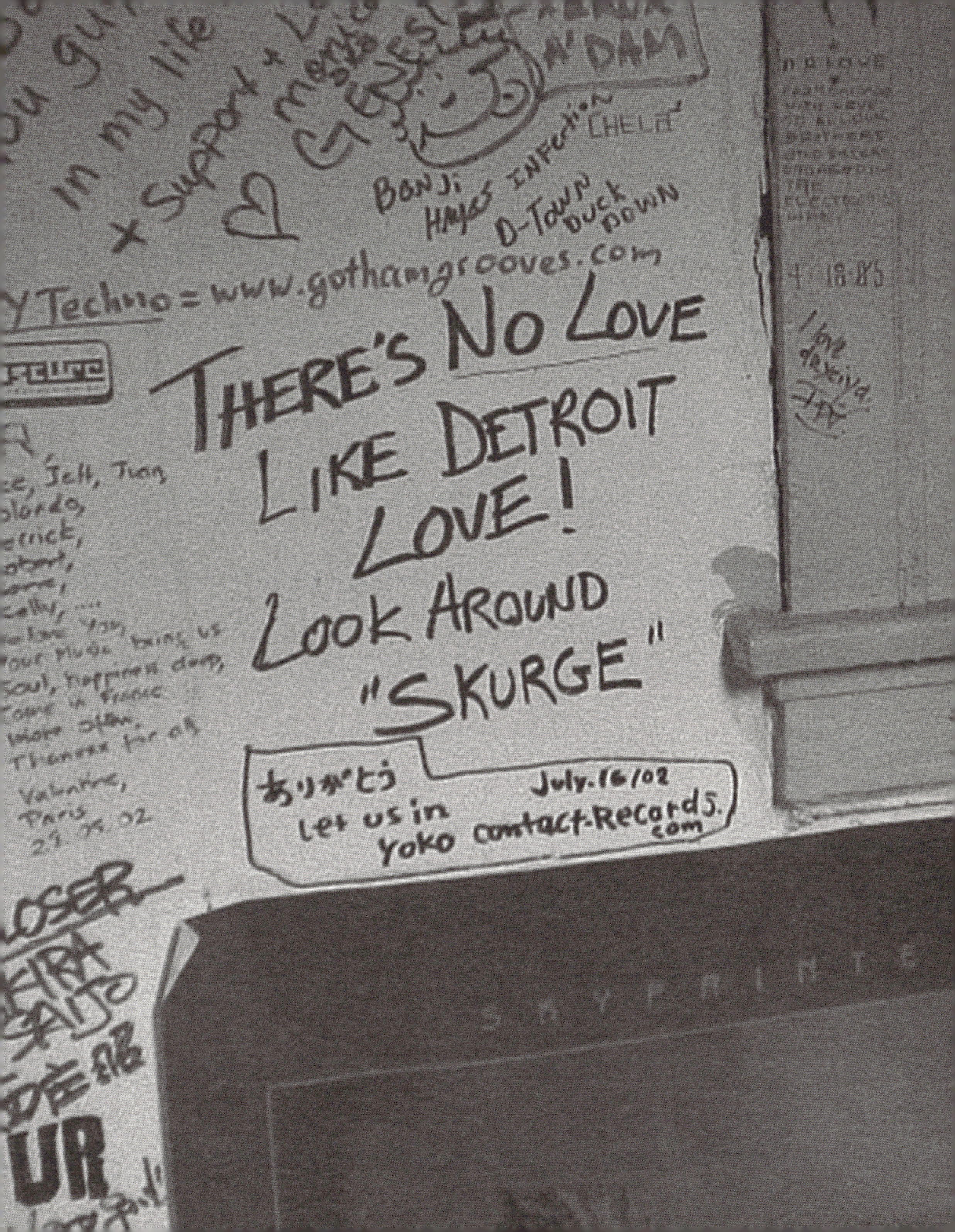

in my life
+ Support + Love
merci
GENESI... A'DAM
BONJi
HAYES Infection CHELA
D-Town DUCK DOWN

Y Techno = www.gothamgrooves.com

THERE'S NO LOVE
LIKE DETROIT
LOVE!
LOOK AROUND
"SKURGE"

ありがとう
let us in
Yoko contact-Records.com
July.16/02

no love

4-18-85

...e, Jeff, Juan
...londa,
...errick,
...
...olly, ...
...love you,
your Music brings us
Soul, happiness deep,
Come in France
more often,
Thanxxx for all
Valentine,
Paris
23.05.02

LOSER
...RA
...JO
...

UR